W9-BLF-793

7/9<

AN AGING POPULATION

OPPOSING VIEWPOINTS®

Other Books of Related Interest

Opposing Viewpoints Series

America Beyond 2001
America's Victims
Biomedical Ethics
Death and Dying
Economics in America
Euthanasia
The Family in America
The Homeless
Health and Fitness
Health Care in America
Population
Poverty
Social Justice
21st Century Earth

Current Controversies Series

Alcoholism
Family Violence
Gambling
Hunger
Reproductive Technologies

AN AGING POPULATION

OPPOSING VIEWPOINTS®

David Bender & Bruno Leone, *Series Editors*

Charles P. Cozic, *Book Editor*

OPPOSING
VIEWPOINTS®
SERIES

Greenhaven Press, Inc., San Diego, CA

Greenhaven Press, Inc.
PO Box 289009
San Diego, CA 92198-9009

Library of Congress Cataloging-in-Publication Data

An aging population : opposing viewpoints / Charles P. Cozic,
    book editor.
        p.   cm. — (Opposing viewpoints series)
    Includes bibliographical references (p.   ) and index.
    ISBN 1-56510-395-5 (lib. bdg. : alk. paper) —
ISBN 1-56510-394-7 (pbk. : alk. paper)
    1. Aged—Government policy—United States. 2. Aged—
United States—Social conditions. 3. Aged—Medical care—
United States. 4. Old age assistance—United States. 5. Aged—
United States—Public opinion. 6. Public opinion—United
States. I. Cozic, Charles P., 1957–   . II. Series: Opposing
viewpoints series (Unnumbered)
HQ1064.U5A6354   1996
305.26'0973—dc20   95-49646
                                                              CIP

Every effort has been made to trace the owners of copyrighted material.

"Congress shall make no law . . .
abridging the freedom of speech,
or of the press."

First Amendment to the U.S. Constitution

The basic foundation of our democracy is the First Amendment
guarantee of freedom of expression. The Opposing Viewpoints
Series is dedicated to the concept of this basic freedom and the
idea that it is more important to practice it than to enshrine it.

Contents

Why Consider Opposing Viewpoints?

> *"The only way in which a human being can make some approach to knowing the whole of a subject is by hearing what can be said about it by persons of every variety of opinion and studying all modes in which it can be looked at by every character of mind. No wise man ever acquired his wisdom in any mode but this."*
>
> John Stuart Mill

In our media-intensive culture it is not difficult to find differing opinions. Thousands of newspapers and magazines and dozens of radio and television talk shows resound with differing points of view. The difficulty lies in deciding which opinion to agree with and which "experts" seem the most credible. The more inundated we become with differing opinions and claims, the more essential it is to hone critical reading and thinking skills to evaluate these ideas. Opposing Viewpoints books address this problem directly by presenting stimulating debates that can be used to enhance and teach these skills. The varied opinions contained in each book examine many different aspects of a single issue. While examining these conveniently edited opposing views, readers can develop critical thinking skills such as the ability to compare and contrast authors' credibility, facts, argumentation styles, use of persuasive techniques, and other stylistic tools. In short, the Opposing Viewpoints Series is an ideal way to attain the higher-level thinking and reading skills so essential in a culture of diverse and contradictory opinions.

In addition to providing a tool for critical thinking, Opposing Viewpoints books challenge readers to question their own strongly held opinions and assumptions. Most people form their opinions on the basis of upbringing, peer pressure, and personal, cultural, or professional bias. By reading carefully balanced opposing views, readers must directly confront new ideas as well as the opinions of those with whom they disagree. This is not to simplistically argue that everyone who reads opposing views will—or should—change his or her opinion. Instead, the series enhances readers' depth of understanding of their own views by encouraging confrontation with opposing ideas. Careful examination of others' views can lead to the readers' understanding of the logical inconsistencies in their own opinions, perspective on why they hold an opinion, and the consideration of the possibility that their opinion requires further evaluation.

Evaluating Other Opinions

To ensure that this type of examination occurs, Opposing Viewpoints books present all types of opinions. Prominent spokespeople on different sides of each issue as well as well-known professionals from many disciplines challenge the reader. An additional goal of the series is to provide a forum for other, less known, or even unpopular viewpoints. The opinion of an ordinary person who has had to make the decision to cut off life support from a terminally ill relative, for example, may be just as valuable and provide just as much insight as a medical ethicist's professional opinion. The editors have two additional purposes in including these less known views. One, the editors encourage readers to respect others' opinions—even when not enhanced by professional credibility. It is only by reading or listening to and objectively evaluating others' ideas that one can determine whether they are worthy of consideration. Two, the inclusion of such viewpoints encourages the important critical thinking skill of objectively evaluating an author's credentials and bias. This evaluation will illuminate an author's reasons for taking a particular stance on an issue and will aid in readers' evaluation of the author's ideas.

As series editors of the Opposing Viewpoints Series, it is our hope that these books will give readers a deeper understanding of the issues debated and an appreciation of the complexity of even seemingly simple issues when good and honest people disagree. This awareness is particularly important in a democratic society such as ours in which people enter into public debate to determine the common good. Those with whom one disagrees should not be regarded as enemies but rather as people whose views deserve careful examination and may shed light on one's own.

Thomas Jefferson once said that "difference of opinion leads to inquiry, and inquiry to truth." Jefferson, a broadly educated man, argued that "if a nation expects to be ignorant and free . . . it expects what never was and never will be." As individuals and as a nation, it is imperative that we consider the opinions of others and examine them with skill and discernment. The Opposing Viewpoints Series is intended to help readers achieve this goal.

David L. Bender & Bruno Leone,
Series Editors

Introduction

"We have to find a way to stop the rising cost of entitlements in this country—and do it soon—or we will be giving our children and grandchildren a burden that will be impossible to bear."

Alan K. Simpson

In 1992, writer Jacob Weisberg observed that his Uncle Marvin, an obstetrician in his late sixties, and his aunt were "eligible for about $24,000 [in Social Security benefits] they don't really need per year, paid for mostly by current workers." Weisberg wrote that if Marvin retired, he would receive the amount he had paid into Social Security in 3.2 years—and would continue receiving Social Security checks for years thereafter.

According to Weisberg, a late-end baby boomer, a growing number of Americans, young and old, have become adversaries in a dispute that may escalate into "not just heightened generational injustice but the real possibility of generational warfare" in the twenty-first century. The main point of contention is that today's seniors receive far more in Social Security and Medicare benefits than they contributed. On the other hand, members of Generation X in their twenties, along with younger Americans, are expected to receive much less than they pay in; some experts predict this group will get nothing at all.

Social Security and Medicare, the federal government's largest entitlement programs, have provided a safety net for older Americans since 1935 and 1965, respectively. Through these programs, eligible seniors are entitled to income and health care services that most would otherwise not receive. But unless reforms are made, the growing population of Americans aged sixty-five or older (from 33.4 million in 1996 to a predicted 59.4 million in 2030) threatens to bankrupt both programs. (As of 1996, proposed federal budget cuts further threatened Medicare benefits.)

Although Social Security payroll taxes from the large population of baby boomers and younger workers virtually guarantees the security of current retirees' benefits, uncertainty clouds the availability of benefits to future retirees. As the elderly population grows, and as the large baby boomer population begins to retire, fewer workers will contribute to Social Security and Medicare while a larger number of seniors will collect benefits. Faced with this scenario, post–baby boomers are pessimistic about the likelihood of claiming the amount in retirement benefits that they have contributed during their working years.

A chief complaint among younger Americans is that seniors' entitlements are an unjust transfer of wealth. They contend that their payroll taxes help fund seniors' Social Security and Medicare benefits while they gain nothing in return. In their book *Retooling Social Security for the Twenty-first Century*, C. Eugene Steuerle and Jon M. Bakija note that the average single male who retired in 1980 will gain $39,000 more in Social Security than his contributions plus the interest they might have earned; a worker retiring in 2030 will lose $62,000. Some experts anticipate the situation growing gloomier, with drastic tax hikes required to pay for retirees' benefits. According to Jon Cowan and Rob Nelson, founders of the now-defunct organization Lead or Leave, "Workers born after 1960 can expect up to 40 percent of their future salaries to go to payroll taxes."

However, many seniors object to the assertion that they are "milking" younger Americans. They argue that they deserve the benefits they have contributed toward, that they are not the greedy recipients of largesse they are portrayed as, and that without Social Security and Medicare, millions of elderly would live in poverty. Describing the impact of Social Security, President Bill Clinton said that in 1985, "for the first time in our history, the percentage of our elderly people who were above the poverty line was better than the percentage of the population as a whole."

Some observers maintain that seniors and Social Security have been made scapegoats for younger Americans' discontent. The real culprit, they argue, is the spendthrift federal government. According to Robert G. Mills, director of the grassroots lobby Council for Government Reform, "Social Security is *not* the problem . . . Congress is! It's the reckless spending habits of the politicians that's to blame, not America's senior citizens." Mills and others submit that wasteful federal programs, not the fiscally sound Social Security system, must be controlled and reformed to balance the budget, thus avoiding tax increases and protecting retirement benefits.

Although generational conflict may have worsened, concern and compassion have not disappeared between young and old. Regardless of their generation, many Americans are sympathetic toward the needs and well-being of their younger or older fellow citizens. While seniors ponder whether they—particularly wealthier individuals—need to sacrifice some benefits, younger Americans understand how crucial Social Security and

13

Medicare are to a growing elderly population. The authors in *An Aging Population: Opposing Viewpoints* examine entitlement benefits and similar aging-related issues in these chapters: How Will an Aging Population Affect America? Should Entitlement Programs for Seniors Be Reformed? What Quality of Life Do Older Americans Face? What Type of Health Care Should the Elderly Receive? How Does Society View Aging and the Elderly? As the "graying of America" proceeds, these questions promise to attract increased consideration.

How Will an Aging Population Affect America?

AN AGING
POPULATION

Chapter Preface

By the year 2030, according to the United Nations, the number of Americans aged sixty-five or older will have more than doubled from its 1995 level of approximately thirty-two million. The swelling of this age group—the result of the aging baby boom generation of Americans born from 1946 to 1964—could have dire consequences for older Americans' entitlement programs, primarily Medicare and Social Security, and could significantly affect younger workers whose taxes help subsidize these benefits. According to former Colorado governor Richard Lamm, "Arguably, the biggest challenge of an aging society is to fund its pension, retirement, and health care systems."

Many experts warn that the threatened viability of such programs could plunge America into economic turmoil. Their chief concerns are federal projections showing that Medicare and Social Security, unless they are reformed, will become bankrupt by 2002 and 2030, respectively. In the words of Rob Nelson, an advocate for Americans in their twenties:

> In 2012, 46 million baby boomers will start [retiring]. At that point, we will face a terrible choice: Double or even triple payroll taxes on my generation and those behind us, or dramatically slash benefits to elderly recipients. The latter course would plunge millions of senior citizens into economic jeopardy. The former will trigger the biggest tax revolt since the Boston Tea Party and lead to a generational war.

Other observers, however, contend that baby boomers and older Americans may stimulate the economy. A September 12, 1994, *Business Week* report stated that "a series of broad, mutually reinforcing changes in the U.S. economy will make an aging population much more of an economic asset." Such changes, the report noted, include higher income and wealth among baby boomers than their parents at the same age and increased productivity from Americans postponing retirement to continue working. According to *Business Week*, "Higher productivity . . . makes it easier to fund the Social Security and healthcare bills that are squeezing America's wallet."

The growing number of older Americans poses many uncertainties. Whether the graying of America will threaten its economy is the focus of the viewpoints in this chapter.

"The young may rightfully resent the burden placed on them by senior citizens."

An Aging Population Will Be Harmful to America

Michael D'Antonio

Government and private-sector policies and programs—including Social Security, Medicare, and pensions—have made the elderly America's most prosperous age group and forced younger and future Americans to pay the bill, Michael D'Antonio argues in the following viewpoint. D'Antonio maintains that younger Americans will be saddled with escalating taxes to pay for the elderly's benefits and will have difficulty providing for their own old age. D'Antonio is a freelance writer and a contributor to the *Los Angeles Times Magazine*.

As you read, consider the following questions:

1. According to D'Antonio, how have poverty rates changed among senior citizens and children?
2. What is often blamed for the decline in the quality of schools, according to the author?
3. What trends could occur in taxes and housing prices, according to D'Antonio?

Excerpted from Michael D'Antonio, "The New Generation Gap," *Los Angeles Times*, March 14, 1993. Reprinted by permission of the author.

The towering billboards on Interstate 95 on the South Florida coast sell a particular kind of dream to a particular kind of buyer. The dream comes true on lush golf courses and in sun-drenched villas. And the buyers, whose permanently smiling faces beam down from these signs, are old, but happy. The hair may be white, but the skin is tanned and smooth. The eyes sparkle with contentment. "Welcome to the club," says the larger-than-life couple on the sign advertising one retirement community.

It is a big club, and a happy one. Millions of senior citizens have settled in Florida and across the Sunbelt into a lifestyle they could not have imagined when they were young. . . .

A Wonderful Life

For many senior citizens, it truly is a wonderful life, especially since someone else is paying much of the bill. Today's elderly, who make up about 12.5% of the population, receive 60% of federal social spending. This is four times as much as is spent on American children. Despite the widely held notion that America neglects the old, the country actually exceeds all of Western Europe and Japan in per capita spending for those over 65. The total, for Social Security, health care and some lesser benefits, is more than $500 billion a year.

All this spending has created a special class of citizens. The elderly are the only age group with universal government health insurance (Medicare) and the only one that receives income assistance—up to $24,500 a year for couples—whether they need it or not. (One million households with $100,000 incomes receive monthly Social Security checks.) Depending on the state they live in, they may also be eligible for age-based tax breaks on property, income and capital gains.

As President Bill Clinton has noted in speeches, the old have bequeathed to the young some daunting economic challenges. The children and grandchildren of today's senior citizens will have to repay the $4.4-trillion national debt, rescue Social Security from potential insolvency and revive an investment-starved economy. Clinton has proposed a combination of new investment and new taxes to start this job, but completing it will be especially difficult because young workers, including college graduates, are making less money. Today's 30-year-old high school graduate earns $3,500 less per year than he would have in 1979. He is also less likely to have health insurance or a pension plan. No wonder that record numbers of young adults remain in their parents' homes: They can't afford to move out.

Conflict Is Brewing

This growing economic gap between the generations has set the stage for a painful political conflict. The young may rightfully resent the burden placed on them by senior citizens who enjoyed the best years of American opportunity and then left them with the world's most-indebted nation, its infrastructures crumbling and social programs teetering on the brink of collapse. Frightened baby boomers—those in their 30s and 40s—have already begun to organize to oppose the powerful senior citizen lobby in Washington. And they have become more vocal in their attacks on a system they say unfairly favors the old. They argue that a country with 20% of its children living in poverty cannot afford to subsidize anyone's country club retirement.

Potential Crises Ahead

Various age-related societal crises could shake the foundation of our nation. The most troublesome of these could be:

• *Age wars*, in which the young retaliate as the old take increasing control of resources (a phenomenon further complicated by the diverse racial/ethnic makeup of the young).

• *Diminishing productivity*, as the result of: 1) young Americans entering the working years unprepared; and 2) tens of millions of non-productive older people draining the economy.

• *Middlescent burn-out*, as baby boomers find themselves supporting nearly everyone.

• *Mass elder poverty*, because too few baby boomers did financial planning.

• *"Gerassic Park,"* as bio-tech radically alters late life disease and aging, sparking battles over who will decide how these technologies are controlled and distributed.

Ken Dychtwald, *Washington Post National Weekly Edition*, May 1-7, 1995.

"Today's elderly, the New Deal generation, have been terrific to themselves," says 40-year-old Paul Hewitt of the National Taxpayers Union, a conservative Washington lobby group. Indeed, if one looks at history through Hewitt's eyes, that group has occupied the most prosperous era in history and has been favored by government initiatives at every step in life. When they needed work, the New Deal gave them work. When they came back from the war, [young Americans] were able to go to college under the GI Bill. Many then bought [their] first home[s] with a subsidized government mortgage. And they sent their children to college with the help of generous loan and subsidy programs that have since dried up.

As today's retirees began to see the end of their working life,

Social Security and Medicare were steadily improved. With the help of large increases in programs for the old, the poverty rate in Senior America has dropped from about 35% in 1960 to 12% in 1993. (In contrast, the percentage of children living in poverty rose from about 14% in 1967 to 20% in 1991.)

Taxes and Wealth

The comfortable retirement of today's elderly has been funded by steadily escalating Social Security taxes. Not coincidentally, Hewitt says, as those taxes have gone up, private savings, which could provide private retirement and investment funds for today's workers, have declined.

The National Taxpayers Union argues that special tax breaks and generous federal programs have evolved from modest supports into a welfare system that shifts enormous amounts of money from the young to the old, many of whom are already rich. One result is that wealth has become more concentrated in the hands of the elderly than at any time in the last two centuries. In fact, New York University economist Edward Wolff estimates that the average household headed by someone 65 or older has a net worth of $258,000. "It's like this one generation won the lottery," says Hewitt. "Naturally, there is a growing sense of resentment" among the younger taxpayers who have to pay out the prizes.

The generations are not yet at war, but the anger bubbles beneath the surface. Privately, some critics of the senior citizens' lobby use terms like "greedy geezers" to describe an elderly population that is wealthier than any other group, but that still resists efforts to limit its government benefits.

Advocates for the elderly say baby boomers don't understand the insecurities of old age. They insist that while Senior America can be described with almost cartoon-like irony, a closer examination yields a much different picture. After all, half of all single women over 65 live on less than $12,000 a year. They don't own golf carts or take Caribbean cruises. And they are terrified of losing the government support—Social Security, housing, medical care—that literally keeps them alive.

Beneath the anger, both sides regard the future with a measure of fear rooted in a Twentieth Century paradox: Science has greatly extended our lives, but we don't know how to pay for these extra years. Billions of dollars are spent each year to gain a few last days of life for elderly Americans. Past generations didn't have to worry about financing this kind of care, or paying for twenty or thirty years of retirement. Today, great numbers of people can expect to spend more time out of the work force—in childhood and old age—than in it. Now, ironically, in addition to fearing death, we all must worry about the cost of living too long.

[Near Palm Beach, Florida,] a small group gathers for drinks and free fried catfish at the Blackwater Bar and Grill, an '80s-style blond-wood fern bar where patrons are greeted by a wooden Indian and a buffet. The core of the local chapter of the American Association of Boomers, they are all in their 30s and 40s, and they are worried. A list of their concerns sounds like Clinton's agenda—health care, the federal debt, Social Security.

The issues may be national in scope, but the anxiety is deeply personal. Thirty-eight-year-old Elaine Davidson wonders when she'll have the money to leave her parents' home. Rick Fanelli, a 41-year-old financial consultant, frets about his personal finances. Hard-pressed to save for retirement and convinced that Social Security will abandon him, Fanelli is counting on an inheritance from his parents to secure his old age. Kathleen Shabotynskyj, 37, chuckles about the slim chance that any of them will ever enjoy the kind of retirement pictured on the billboards out on I-95. Her own parents, Ann and Jerry Irving, lead this kind of life in a South Florida development called Martin Downs, their days revolving around the local country club. While Shabotynskyj doesn't begrudge her parents' pleasures, she believes their lifestyle is a fading dream. "I'm never going to be able to retire like my parents," she says, "unless I move to the Bahamas."

Doing Without

Not one of the boomers gathered around the table is counting on collecting anything from Social Security. In a 1991 poll, 90% of Americans ages 30 to 39 said they did not expect to get back what they are paying into the system. It is impossible to say whether this fear is justified, but it is likely that Social Security benefits will be scaled back. And today's young aren't likely to get the kind of generous pensions that their parents' generation received, either. In fact, so many companies have failed to adequately fund pension programs that the Pension Benefit Guaranty Corp., which ensures that retirees will be paid, is expected to run deficits well into the twenty-first century. Among the companies with underfunded pension plans are giants such as Chrysler, General Motors and Bethlehem Steel. If just one goes out of business, the taxpayers could be stuck with the bill for billions in pension obligations.

Because the Social Security and pension systems both face problems, the boomers are under pressure to provide for their own old age. But though they know they should be putting their own money away for the future, many are hard-pressed by the high cost of housing and health care. Since the '70s, many employers have cut back on health insurance, while the cost of health care has exploded. Those in today's work force must labor harder and longer than their parents to achieve the same standard of living.

A Greater Predicament

This predicament is more prevalent among those born after 1955. Many of their older brothers and sisters were able to buy homes in the late 1970s, and they benefited from the real estate inflation of the 1980s. But those who entered the job market in the recession-prone '70s did not get rich in real estate. Instead, they watched interest rates soar and the price of even a starter home float beyond their grasp. The traditional cornerstone of middle-class security was eluding them. Slowly, they began to realize that they would be the first young Americans who might not do better in life than their parents, a theme Clinton played to during the campaign.

"By the time they were my age, my parents had a custom-built, four-bedroom house and seven kids," notes Shabotynskyj, who is an office worker. Today she and her husband, who works in the computer field, occupy a tiny two-bedroom home with their 4-year-old son. With a full-time job and no maternity benefits, Shabotynskyj is not sure whether she'll have more children. She expects to work until she's at least 67, and even then she fears that retirement will be a struggle. Things will be even worse, she fears, if the American economy continues to lose high-paying manufacturing jobs and fails to educate the young so they can be productive adults.

In Florida and elsewhere, the cost of Medicare and the senior-citizen vote are often blamed for limiting school spending and helping to speed the collapse of urban school districts. Across the nation, districts are cutting teachers' salaries and increasing class sizes. Meanwhile, funding for day care centers remains inadequate. At the Bright Beginnings Day Care Center in West Palm Beach, for example, there are about fifty names on the waiting list for thirty-two subsidized slots. Countywide, more than one thousand eligible low-income children are on waiting lists.

Young parents see underfunded, overcrowded schools and inadequate day care as evidence of generational inequity and another warning sign. Looking ahead to the twenty-first century, it is hard to imagine how an undereducated, under-parented nation of fast-food workers will generate the kind of growth and tax revenues needed to deal with the national debt and expanding social needs. "That's why our age group has to begin to put pressure on the politicians now," says Shabotynskyj. "We can't stay out of politics anymore."

That sentiment led Dallas-area accountant Karen Meredith to form the American Association of Boomers. The four-year-old group already has about 26,000 members in chapters scattered nationwide, and Social Security is at the top of their agenda. Government officials raised taxes for the program from 1983 to 1993 to build a trust fund surplus to cover the seventy-seven million baby boomers when they retire in the twenty-first century. But according to Meredith, the surplus is a mirage.

"First of all, there really is no 'trust fund' for Social Security," says Meredith. In fact, Social Security has always depended on current taxes paid by younger workers to finance retirement benefits. The average worker retiring today gets back all he or she contributed in less than six years, and may go on collecting benefits indefinitely. "The second problem is there really is no cash surplus being built up," she adds. Indeed, the government has been borrowing from the surplus to reduce the size of the annual budget deficit, giving the Social Security system special non-negotiable bonds that the Treasury promises to repay, by passing the debt on to taxpayers. But even if the payments are made, Social Security officials admit that without major reforms, the system will run out of money just as the last of the boomers retire.

When Social Security was created in 1935, relatively few people could expect to live long enough to collect. And in the beginning, there were fifty-five workers to support each retiree, so taxes for the old-age program could be kept low. Today, the average American will live to be at least 75, and the ratio of workers to retirees is about 3 to 1. It is as if a group of grandchildren agreed to support an aging grandmother who then proceeded to outlive them. As the years go by, there are fewer grandchildren shouldering the burden, and granny's expenses, especially health care, continue to rise. At least a third of all taxpayers pay more into Social Security and Medicare than they pay in federal income tax.

"We just can't go on like this indefinitely," Meredith argues. "There have to be some changes made, soon." Old-age benefits will have to be reduced, she says, and the elderly will likely have to pay for more of their own medical care. "This is something a lot of people don't want to hear," she says. "But at some point, fairness has to be considered." . . .

Boomers and Elders

Boomers who feel financial pressure today should expect more stress in the future, warns Hewitt of the National Taxpayers Union. Huge federal deficits will require several rounds of federal tax increases. At the same time, some analysts are expecting a further, steep decline in housing prices after large numbers of older citizens begin putting their homes on the market in the mid-'90s. These sellers, who will need cash for retirement, are likely to create an oversupply that may drive prices further down. "We're in an interregnum right now, before an incredible fall," says Hewitt. "It could also have a serious effect on the financial sector, because it is so tied up in real estate."

In this harsh new world, boomers and their elders may find comfort in coming together. They could re-create some of the traditional relationships that have seemed to disappear in modern times.

David Demko, a gerontologist and author of a syndicated advice column for senior citizens, predicts that small group homes for senior citizens, which are already sprouting in some places, will become common by the year 2000. Extended families may also come back into vogue during the decades ahead. In these intergenerational households, senior citizens who are welcomed into their children's homes will be relied on to care for grandchildren. Middle-aged boomers will in turn provide more support for their mothers and fathers even as they struggle to save for their own uncertain old age.

This new, old-fashioned lifestyle will reduce the isolation of the old and the young, an isolation so real in South Florida that senior citizens often ask new mothers not to take their crying babies out of restaurants because they enjoy hearing the sound.

"Independence is wonderful, but it can be taken to the extreme, which is isolation," says Demko. Indeed, since the 1960s and the development of retirement communities, old and young have been leading ever more separate lives. Along the way, young people have been denied everyday contact with the realities of aging and the old have lost touch with the young.

But even Demko, who advocates this way of life, has no illusions. "Families like the TV Waltons, where everyone lived together, didn't all love it. But people had to come together, out of necessity, and they made it work."

"Those who wring their hands in despair for the calamity that will eventually befall the baby boom in old age should relax a bit."

An Aging Population May Not Be Harmful to America

Charles F. Longino Jr.

Although the number of elderly Americans will reach a record high in the near future, they may not have a detrimental effect on America, Charles F. Longino Jr. argues in the following viewpoint. Longino maintains that a decline in disability, improvements in diet, and opportunities for living independently are some of the factors that indicate that America may not suffer from an increasingly aged population. Longino is a sociology professor at Wake Forest University in Winston-Salem, North Carolina, and a contributing editor for *American Demographics* magazine.

As you read, consider the following questions:

1. In Longino's opinion, why are women a greater health concern than men?
2. How has Americans' food consumption changed, according to Longino?
3. According to the author, how has sensory technology helped the aged?

Charles F. Longino Jr., "Myths of an Aging America," *American Demographics* magazine, August 1994; ©1994. Reprinted with permission.

If demographers ever sat around campfires telling scary stories, their favorite would be called "The Demographic Imperative." It's a dark and terrible story about the transformation of a carefree, youthful America into a nation of ancient, sickly wretches with no one to care for them. Like the best scary stories, it is firmly based in fact. But like many horror stories, it's not so scary when viewed in the proper light.

The story begins at the dawn of the twentieth century, when most Americans were rural dwellers under age 25. Only 3.1 million Americans—just 4 percent of the total population—were aged 65 and older. The life expectancy of a newborn white child was only about 50 years then, and it was less than 35 for blacks and others.

Then a miracle happened. In just three decades, the average life expectancy for whites shot up to about 60, and the life expectancy for others approached 50. The number of elderly people more than doubled to 6.7 million, about 5 percent of the total population. By this time, the largest share of Americans were urban dwellers. With the Great Depression in full swing, they were hungry for a better life. In response to the growing needs of the elderly, the Social Security Act passed in 1935.

Now the story moves forward another thirty years, to 1960. While America entered a new cultural phase that worshipped youth, its elderly population more than doubled again. There were 16.7 million Americans aged 65 and older in 1960, about 9 percent of the total population. Life expectancy reached about 70 for whites and over 60 for others.

Anticipating Hardship

As the baby-boom generation continued to swell hospital nurseries, demographers began worrying that the miracle of longer life might turn into an uncontrollable beast. They began talking about a "population bomb" and anticipating the hardship that growing numbers of elderly Americans would place upon society. More than two-thirds of Americans lived in urban areas in 1960. In response to heightened concern for the plight of the elderly, the Medicare Amendment to the Social Security Act passed in 1965.

In the last thirty or so years, the elderly population has nearly doubled again. Now 31 million people, or 12 percent of the total population, are aged 65 and older. The American landscape has changed dramatically since 1900: the total population has more than tripled, and urban areas are now home to more than 75 percent of Americans.

In another thirty-five years, the elderly population should double again. The Census Bureau anticipates that sixty-two million people, or almost one in five Americans, will be aged 65 and older by 2025. And by 2045, the elderly population will reach seventy-seven million, more than the total population of the United States in 1900. And now comes the scary part of the demographic imperative.

An Overwhelming Burden?

At this point in the story, demographers lower their voices and begin talking about the changing characteristics of the elderly population. As they speak, shivers run down the spines of spellbound listeners. The elderly population is not only growing rapidly, it's also getting older.

The oldest old, aged 85 and older, are increasing at a faster rate than the total elderly population. In 1990, fewer than one in ten elderly persons was aged 85 or older. By 2045, the oldest old will be one in five. Increasing longevity and the steady movement of baby boomers into this oldest age group will drive this trend.

The demographic imperative reminds us that disability increases as people age. Only 9 percent of people aged 65 to 69 need help with any personal care, such as eating, bathing, going to the bathroom, or dressing; 45 percent of people aged 85 and older need help. And because women live longer than men, many of the oldest old are widows. There are 1.5 women for every man aged 65 and older. Among the oldest old, there are 2.6 women for every man.

Even though women live longer, they are more vulnerable than men to chronic conditions. And their low incomes make their medical care a public rather than a private issue. When these grim statistics are projected into the future, many researchers conclude that Americans are growing older and becoming more sickly. They worry that Americans will be less capable of caring for themselves, both physically and economically.

Finding able-bodied people to provide that care could be a problem, because the supply of caregivers is not keeping pace with the growth in the older population. The number of elderly persons for every one hundred adults of working age (aged 18 to 64) is called the old-age dependency ratio. In 1990, there were twenty elderly persons for every one hundred working-aged adults. But the burden of caring for the elderly may become much heavier as the baby-boom generation enters its retirement years. When the youngest boomers approach retirement age in 2025, there will be thirty-two elderly persons for every one hundred people of working age.

The rising cost of caring for the elderly deepens the darkness of the demographic imperative. Without serious health-care reform, the United States could spend 20 percent of its Gross Domestic Product on health care by the year 2000. Currently, more than one-third of total health-care expenditures are spent on the 12 percent of the population aged 65 and older. And public funds are the major source of payment for the elderly population.

The deepening gloom of the demographic imperative is global in proportions. Rising health-care costs were absorbed in the growing national economy of the 1950s and 1960s. But national economic trends became starkly negative during the late 1970s and 1980s. The industrialized world is caught up in an extended period of recession, economic restructuring, and stagnation. The results are lower tax revenues and greater demands on the national treasury.

The demographic imperative concludes that tomorrow's elderly will be whiplashed by converging trends. Their numbers and proportions are growing inexorably as the wealth of the nation deteriorates. Our already serious long-term-care problem promises to grow to crisis proportions. In the horrifying final vision of the demographic imperative, the United States becomes a twenty-first-century Calcutta, with futuristic Mother Teresas ministering to the dying elderly on the streets of Cincinnati.

The Wild Card

Many researchers have become accustomed to the story of the demographic imperative. In fact, they're so convinced of it that anyone who would question its dire predictions is in danger of being dismissed as a crackpot. Almost everyone foresees that the demand for long-term care will increase, but there is room for disagreement about how much it will increase—and how to address the problem. The story of the demographic imperative and its many depressing details indeed deserves to be challenged.

The biggest problem with the demographic imperative is that it ignores generational effects. Yet generational change will transform the older population, the caregiving population, and society as a whole. Researchers have become fixated on certain age groups. They characterize the population aged 85 and older as a high-risk group and underestimate differences in coming generations. Yet it is likely that several factors will work to reduce disability among the elderly, including improved health, new forms of service delivery, and improved technology.

Will baby boomers, who popularized healthy lifestyles, be healthier in old age? Since 1953, per capita tobacco consumption has declined by 40 percent in the United States. Butter consumption is down by one-third, whole milk and cream are down one-fourth, and saturated animal fats for cooking are down 40 percent. Consumption of vegetable oils and fish has increased. These behaviors may cut the rates of chronic diseases in old age, potentially reducing the use of health services and lengthening the average person's productive life.

These positive trends may already be paying healthy dividends. The prevalence of chronic disability among the elderly declined 4 percent between 1984 and 1989. Furthermore, the declines were greatest among those aged 85 and older. These improvements may be due to increasing levels of education and income, as a new generation moves into the eldest age group.

Of course, modest declines in disability will not be enough to offset the increases in disability caused by the growth of the elderly population. But even though absolute numbers of the chronically disabled will certainly continue to rise, the expansion may not be as great as the catastrophe some demographic doomsayers predict.

Improvements in Health and Health Care Costs

Because of better early health care, nutrition, and increased health awareness, the health of the elderly has shown gradual improvement in recent years. Studies show morbidity declined, on average, 6 percent per decade from 1910 to 1985. My own research suggests that there have been declines in chronic morbidity and disability in the elderly population and greater use of special equipment and housing. Less dependence in general, and use of special equipment by those disabled, means improved health and less reliance on costly personal assistance. This, in turn, slows the climb of health care costs. Well-targeted investments might further aid this trend, reduce health care costs and improve the social autonomy of the elderly.

Reduced health care costs aren't the only benefit of a healthier older population. Older people will also be able to lead more productive, vital lives, though a whole new range of measures must be established to quantify the exact benefits.

Kenneth Manton, *Washington Post National Weekly Edition*, May 1-7, 1995.

Another progressive and rapid change among the elderly is their increasing desire to live independently of children and other relatives. The independent elderly are less likely to use caregivers and more likely to use paid help or products and services to get what they need. In 1990, about nine million Americans aged 65 and older lived alone. By 2010, that number is expected to approach thirteen million, according to *American Demographics* projections. Three out of four of these householders will be women. But older men living alone—especially those aged 75 and older—are a rapidly growing segment.

Today, elderly people in their 60s and 70s are well-endowed with family resources—because they are the parents of the baby boom. The supply of family caregivers will decline as the baby-boom generation retires, because this group has fewer children. On the other hand, the burden of caregiving will be slightly offset by future declines in childbearing. In 1990, there were forty-two children under age 18 for every one hundred adults aged 18 to 64. By 2025, that number will slip to forty-one.

Assistive Devices

The depletion of caregivers is being accelerated by the continued movement of women out of the home and into the labor force. Yet gerontologists have not detected a shift from family caregivers to paid caregivers; instead, the use of assistive devices and housing modifications is rising sharply, while the long-term use of personal assistants alone is declining significantly.

Greater residential independence, combined with the development and use of personal-assistance technologies, seem to be part of a modern elderly person's long-term adaptive process. Unless there is some kind of interdependence that preserves self-respect and self-determination, dependency on family members or others will be a far less attractive alternative than technically supported self-care for those who can afford it. As the high-risk population grows—and the horror story tells us that it surely will—a marketplace for assistive technology will grow with it.

Sensory technology, such as eyeglasses and hearing aids, has been around for a long time. Now, electric wheelchairs, sensory aids for telephone equipment, voice-activated devices for adjusting lighting and temperature at home, and biomedical devices to strengthen or replace legs, arms, toes, and fingers are becoming commonplace. This category of technology will be a growth industry in the next century as the baby boom reaches advanced age.

In the twenty-first century, older Americans may be better prepared to live independently. Incremental increases in Social Security will protect older householders from inflation and recessions. Aging baby-boom women will also have resources their mothers never had. Because they delayed marriage and experienced high divorce rates, many have lived independently for years. They are used to keeping their homes, managing their money, and tending to emergencies by themselves. Virtually all baby-boom women have worked outside the home for at least part of their lives, and many will have their own pension incomes.

Defusing the Problem

Americans are notorious for addressing problems only when they become national crises. The Social Security adjustments in the early 1980s averted such a crisis; the health-care reform legislation of the early 1990s is another example. When the long-term-care crisis mounts in the twenty-first century, the U.S. public will come to the rescue by advancing policies to reform caregiving. Even in the next decade, we will see policy discussion that will set the stage for those dramatic events. The ideas that will become a part of the national debate in 2010 are forming today.

Businesses can also help to defuse the demographic imperative. Private firms that produce and distribute services and goods to enhance independence longer into old age will find growing markets, and the competition they generate will make these products available at a decreasing cost. This will primarily benefit the smaller generation following the boomers. And because the baby boom came later in many Third World countries than in the United States, overseas markets will provide expanded opportunities for assistive devices long after the American baby-boom generation is gone.

Those who wring their hands in despair for the calamity that will eventually befall the baby boom in old age should relax a bit. Despite their competitive struggle for education, jobs, and housing, boomers have always had political clout. When they turned 18, they got the vote. Boomers stopped the Vietnam War, relaunched the feminist movement, celebrated the first Earth Day, and raised the drinking age before their kids became teenagers. In 2010, the baby boom will demand changes in long-term-care policy. They will want better support in their old age, and they will have it.

When Chicken Little said that the sky was falling, he lost credibility. The same fate may await those who crow about the demographic imperative without questioning its assumptions. The imperative is frequently used as a strategy to keep public support high for special interests that serve the elderly. These interests will certainly have a place in America's future, but they may not bear as much of a burden as the demographic imperative now assigns them. The future may not be quite as scary as we think.

"It is undeniable that the cost of the U.S. government's kind treatment of today's elderly will be borne on the backs of tomorrow's children."

An Economic Burden Is Being Placed on Future Generations

Laurence J. Kotlikoff and Jagadeesh Gokhale

U.S. government policies regarding taxes and benefits favor older Americans and will place a disproportionate economic burden on future generations, Laurence J. Kotlikoff and Jagadeesh Gokhale argue in the following viewpoint. The authors maintain that current Americans are not paying as much in taxes as they receive in government benefits. They warn that unless Americans pay more in taxes now, net tax rates for future Americans will double those of today's citizens. Kotlikoff is an economics professor at Boston University. Gokhale is an economist at the Federal Reserve Bank in Cleveland.

As you read, consider the following questions:

1. According to the authors, why has consumption among the elderly increased?
2. What two changes in U.S. fiscal policy would lower the tax rates of future generations, according to Kotlikoff and Gokhale?
3. How could the low rate of U.S. saving affect children in the future, in the authors' opinion?

Excerpted from Laurence J. Kotlikoff and Jagadeesh Gokhale, "Passing the Generational Buck." Reprinted, with permission, from the *Public Interest*, no. 114, Winter 1994, p. 73ff; ©1994, National Affairs, Inc.

Are today's children being treated fairly compared with other generations? To address this issue, we will rely on a new method called generational accounting, which compares the "lifetime net tax burden" (taxes paid minus transfer payments received) of different generations. [Transfer payments are a redistribution of income to recipients deemed needy or worthy.] With its lifetime perspective, generational accounting overcomes the difficulty encountered with the usual comparisons between two generations, namely that the two generations are at different stages of their life cycles.

To understand this difficulty, imagine a country with a long-standing policy of transfer payments to children, financed by taxes on the elderly. While the usual comparison would suggest that children are being treated favorably compared to the elderly, such a comparison ignores the fact that the elderly received the same when they were young, as well as the fact that the children will pay the same taxes when they are old. Thus from a lifetime perspective, the children are being treated just as favorably as the elderly.

How are children in America actually being treated compared to adults and the elderly? . . .

Consumption Then and Now

One way to assess the change in living standards of all children vis-a-vis all adults is to consider changes over time in the age-consumption profile. Consider, for example, the average consumption of children aged 10 versus the average consumption of adults aged 70. In 1972–73, the consumption of children aged 10 averaged 37 percent of the consumption of 70-year-olds. But by 1987–90, it averaged only 31 percent. Thus, the consumption of 10-year-olds relative to that of 70-year-olds fell by over 16 percent across the two periods.

What explains the recent increase in the relative consumption of the elderly? The answer is that over the past twenty or so years their income has grown much more rapidly than that of other age groups. In 1968, income per elderly household averaged 43 percent of income per household aged 35–44. By 1984, this figure had risen to an average of 54 percent. Thus the income of the elderly relative to that of households aged 35–44 rose by 26 percent over the sixteen-year period. It rose by an even larger percentage—45 percent—relative to that of households aged 25–34.

If anything, these numbers are likely to understate the recent growth in the relative income of the elderly, because they do not include the value of government-provided health care benefits, such as those from Medicare and Medicaid.

Has the government helped to offset or worsen these trends?

One way to approach this question is to consider the government's direct transfer payments to different age groups, as well as the taxes the government collects from the various groups.

A Redistribution of Wealth

How could anyone begrudge his parents and grandparents, who survived the Great Depression, won the Second World War and put us [baby boomers] through college, a few breaks [economic benefits and monetary discounts] at a time when their earned incomes are declining or terminating. Only a Grinch. But a look at the larger picture shows more than a few favors for old folks. It demonstrates a dramatic, socially troublesome redistribution of wealth from America's young to America's old. In 1991, $74 billion in Social Security and Medicare benefits went to people like my aunt and uncle with household incomes in excess of $50,000. For a little perspective, that's nearly as much as the total budgets of the departments of Education and Agriculture and the Environmental Protection Agency combined.

Jacob Weisberg, *Worth*, June/July 1992.

Older Americans receive transfer payments that are many times greater than those received by children. In 1970, for example, the average transfer payment made to 70-year-old women was $5,120, while the average transfer payment to 10-year-old girls was just $350. In 1990, the comparable figures were $10,467 paid to 70-year-old women and $410 paid to 10-year-old girls.

The elderly do, of course, pay far more in taxes than children, even if we impute sales and excise tax payments to children. In 1990, for example, the average tax payment of 70-year-old women was $7,262, while the average tax payment of 10-year-old girls was $799. However, if one subtracts these tax payments from the transfer payments received, the resulting net payment figures, $3,205 and ⁻$389, respectively, still show that the elderly benefit much more than children from government transfers and taxes. . . .

Net Tax Rates

Generational accounting can help us assess the true generational equity of government policy. Generational accounts reflect what members of a generation can expect to pay, on average, in net taxes (tax payments minus transfers received) over their lifetimes. Such accounts can be used to compare the government's treatment of different generations, since they take account of all taxes and transfers over the life cycle.

What generational policy is actually in place? One way to determine this is to examine the net tax rate of each generation: the average amount of taxes a generation will pay minus the benefits it will receive, all divided by its lifetime income. This figure has risen significantly over time, increasing from 22 percent for the generation born in 1900 to 34 percent for the generation born in 1991.

Gross tax and transfer rates have also risen over this period. The lifetime transfer rate (transfers divided by income) nearly quadrupled between 1900 and 1991, from 3.3 percent in 1900 to 12.2 percent in 1991. The increase was more rapid, in both relative and absolute terms, for the generations born before World War II than for those born after.

Because of the need to pay for higher transfers and government purchases, the gross tax rate has also risen in the past two decades, while the net tax rate (taxes minus transfers) has stayed fairly constant. The gross tax rate is 25 percent for the generation born in 1900, and 46 percent for the generation born in 1991.

What Future Americans Will Pay

We've not yet discussed the tax rates to be paid by future generations. Some generation must pay the government's bills, and if current generations do not pay as much in taxes as they receive in benefits, future generations will be forced to cover the difference.

Unless present-day Americans are made to pay more, on net, over their remaining lives, future Americans will face lifetime net tax rates of 71 percent—more than twice the lifetime net tax rate to be paid by Americans born in 1991. This figure assumes that the generations living now will continue paying no more than they are at present. Of course this is just an assumption. It is made not because of its infallibility, but rather to illustrate the extent of the imbalance in U.S. generational policy. As we discuss in the next subsection, other assumptions about the evolution of future U.S. fiscal policy lead to lower lifetime net tax rates for future generations, albeit at the price of higher rates for current generations, particularly younger ones.

Possible Policy Changes

Today's American children face much higher lifetime net tax rates than do today's elderly. The generation born in 1991, for example, faces a lifetime net tax rate that is 27 percent greater than that of the generation born in 1920. This discrepancy would be exacerbated by changes in U.S. fiscal policy that might be taken to prevent future generations from paying over 70 percent of their lifetime net incomes to the government.

Consider two possible changes in U.S. fiscal policy. The first of these involves placing a cap from 1993 to 2004 on all federal spending on mandatory programs, with the exception of Social Security and deposit insurance. Medicare and Medicaid are the two programs that would experience the largest cuts. The second possible policy is a surtax on the federal individual income tax, which would last from 1993 to 2004 and produce the same deficit reduction as the cap.

Both of these policies would dramatically lower the lifetime net tax rates of future generations. Under the mandatory cap policy, future generations would pay only 41 percent of their lifetime incomes to the government. Under the surtax policy, future generations would pay 46 percent. While these means of bringing U.S. generational policy into closer balance are good for future generations, they would of course harm current generations. The surtax, for example, would force children born in 1991 to pay 40 percent of their lifetime incomes to the government rather than 34 percent. The cap and surtax would also raise the lifetime net tax rate of today's older Americans. If the surtax were implemented, there would be a 53 percent difference in the lifetime net tax rates of children born in 1991 and those born in 1920.

Generational Equity

Is it fair that today's children may have to hand upwards of 40 percent of their lifetime income over to the government while their grandparents will end up paying just over a quarter of their lifetime income? The answer depends on several factors. First, today's children will, it appears, receive more services in the form of educational expenditures and public goods than will today's elderly. Second, certain types of contributions made by today's elderly, such as fighting World War II, are not factored into the analysis. Consideration of these special contributions might suggest a lower lifetime tax rate for the current elderly. Third, the steep increase in lifetime tax rates may be justified to the extent that society's notion of generational equity entails equalizing the after-tax incomes of current and future generations.

If, however, society's notion of generational equity entails extracting an equal proportional sacrifice from each generation, these numbers are highly discomforting. They reveal a U.S. generational policy that will burden today's children much more than today's elderly. Tomorrow's children, meanwhile, are likely to be burdened even more.

Regardless of how one views the data presented above, it is worth pointing out that they are likely to understate the generational differences in economic well-being generated by U.S. fiscal policy. The reason is that every tax dollar the government has failed to collect from past and present generations has meant another dollar available to finance additional consumption. In consuming more, these generations have raised total U.S. consumption and lowered total saving. While there are certainly other factors beyond generational policy at play in explaining the recent decline in U.S. saving, generational policy has surely played a significant role. The United States is now saving at record low levels. In 1991, for example, the U.S. saving rate was only 1.7 percent—dramatically lower than the almost 9 percent rate observed during the years 1950–1969.

Lower saving means lower investment, which means a slower rate of growth of the U.S. capital stock relative to the U.S. labor force. Since labor productivity depends on the amount of capital available per worker and since wages reflect labor productivity, the decline in saving is responsible for lower U.S. wage growth. It is also responsible for raising the return to capital, since it has made capital more scarce relative to the other factor of production—labor—than would otherwise have been the case. Those who have been harmed most by slower wage growth are today's young and middle-aged workers, who have experienced very slow growth in their hourly pay over the past two decades. If the low rate of U.S. saving continues, today's children will also experience very slow wage growth once they enter the workforce. Since the late 1970s, on the other hand, the return to capital has been quite high, and the main beneficiaries of this high return have been today's elderly, who are the primary owners of capital.

Passing the Buck

A significant body of evidence points to a deterioration in the living standard of children relative to that of adults. There also has been a rapid increase in the lifetime net tax rates of American generations born through the course of the twentieth century. Americans born at the turn of the twentieth century paid just over a fifth of their lifetime incomes to the government. Those born at the beginning of the the twenty-first century are likely to pay well over half of their lifetime net incomes to the government.

Does this considerable disparity imply that U.S. fiscal policy is generationally inequitable? The answer depends on society's notion of generational equity, on society's assessment of the special contributions that particular generations have made to the country, and on the level of benefits being provided to different generations as a result of government purchases of goods and services. But it is undeniable that the cost of the U.S. government's kind treatment of today's elderly will be borne on the backs of tomorrow's children.

"We might say that each infant born today is given a nest egg of government saving bonds, or Treasury bills, notes, and bonds equal to $50,000. Is that a burden?"

An Economic Burden Is Not Being Placed on Future Generations

Robert Eisner

In the following viewpoint, Robert Eisner asserts that "generational accountants"—those who warn that financial debts will accumulate and be passed on to future generations—incorrectly calculate the economic burden on future Americans. Eisner contends that generational accountants' measurements are too narrow to accurately portray the effects of current policies on the next generations and that they do not factor in government spending that will benefit these future U.S. citizens. Eisner, professor emeritus at Northwestern University in Evanston, Illinois, and former president of the American Economic Association, is the author of *The Misunderstood Economy: What Counts and How to Count It*.

As you read, consider the following questions:

1. According to Eisner, on what do projections of tax increases depend?
2. What types of government spending may benefit future generations, according to Eisner?

Robert Eisner, "The Grandkids Can Relax," *Wall Street Journal*, November 9, 1994.

> Every newborn baby starts out with a debt of over $50,000 be-
> cause he or she will owe that much more in taxes than he or
> she will ever receive in government benefits.
>
> —*Warren Rudman and Paul Tsongas, for The Concord Coalition*

> If there is no change in the net taxes paid by current genera-
> tions, future generations will have to pay net taxes equal to
> 71% of their lifetime incomes.
>
> —*Laurence Kotlikoff, in* Generational Accounting

There's a new hot topic in the economics profession that's receiving considerable attention in policy-making circles. It has
great appeal to those gloom-and-doomers who don't find the
conventional budget-deficit paranoia sufficiently extreme. Such
people can be found in both political parties.

Generational Accounting

It's called generational accounting. It is grounded in the idea
that debts piled up by the current generations are being passed
wholesale to future generations. Assuming that government will
eventually pay all its bills, the proponents of this view measure
how much the burden on each generation will be in "net taxes."
If those alive now are paying less, those yet to be born will have
to pay more.

And the numbers that the generational-accounting economists
come up with—people like Mr. Kotlikoff of Boston University
and Alan Auerbach of the University of Pennsylvania and Jagadeesh Gokhale of the Federal Reserve Bank of Cleveland—are
indeed shocking. Mr. Kotlikoff argues that the prospective net
tax rate for future generations is up to 82%; it would have been
93.7% without the Clinton deficit-reduction package. Even with
the package, future generations will pay 126% more in taxes
than those currently alive!

Technical Problems

Generational accounting figured in the political debate that
culminated in the November 1994 election, at least implicitly,
since the deficit hemmed in electioneering claims about taxes
and benefits. The GOP's [Grand Old Party's] Contract With
America [ten reforms pursued in 1995 by the Republican-led
Congress] proclaimed support for a balanced-budget amendment, while promising to cut taxes and raise military spending.
The Democrats charged that its fulfillment would require huge
sacrifices in Medicare and retirement benefits for the elderly.
Budget Director Alice Rivlin's "Big Choices" memo specifically
mentioned the possibility—later rejected by President Clinton—
of curbing elderly benefits to hold the deficit in check.

As economics, though, generational accounting has a lot of technical problems. And it leads us away from some real issues, especially the amount of saving and investment that will determine how big a pie the economy will produce for our children and grandchildren.

A true look at generational accounts would have to offer a much fuller picture than its advocates currently provide. It would have to tell us what we are providing each generation in the real capital—public and private, human and nonhuman—on which each generation's total production and earnings will depend. The narrow government accounts presented by Mr. Kotlikoff and his associates might then play a role, although one that is far from obvious. Those accounts do not show what government is doing to provide public investment and, in its financing or taxing, what government is doing to encourage or discourage private saving and investment.

Consider the basic "finding" of the generational accountants, that future generations—those born from now on—will have to pay enormously more in taxes than those already living. That is based on the assumption that, given projected expenditures, taxes will have to be increased and all such increases will be borne by those yet to be born; everyone now alive, including one-year-olds, will have no increase in taxes.

Higher Taxes

This indeed is a strange scenario. At some point in the future, one or 10 or 20 years from now, we will be forced to see the error of our ways and raise taxes or cut benefits. But at that point, it is posited, we would impose these burdens only on those coming into the world after 1994. We would presumably put our birth dates on our tax returns and have a surtax if we were born too late, and we would similarly be denied entitlement benefits still enjoyed by those born a bit earlier.

If, more realistically, an increase in net taxes—either higher taxes or lower government benefit payments—were at some point implemented for all, regardless of age or generation, the difference between generational tax burdens would largely disappear, and with it most of the dramatic conclusions of "generational accounting."

Further, generational accountants arrive at large prospective tax rates in part because they take the present value of all net taxes plus the existing government debt and divide the sum by the present value of only labor income, which is perhaps two-thirds of total gross income (which also includes investment income and other things). All this is sensitive to interest rates, which the authors project out at a real rate of 6%. At lower rates (which are likely)—corresponding to what might be applied to service of the government debt—the tax rates and differentials are markedly less.

Another problem: The projections of large increases in taxes depend on uncertain forecasts well into the 21st century of what will be happening to population, productivity and health costs. The possibility that in 2050 we would need higher taxes to finance Social Security payments to retirees then is hardly any reason to raise taxes now. Retirees in 2050 will be living off the production of those working in 2050, and their benefits will have to be financed by them. Higher taxes now might just stifle the economy and slow our long-run growth, thus raising future tax burdens.

Elderly Americans Will Not Be an Economic Burden

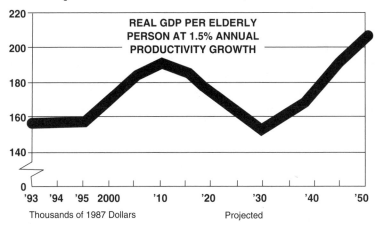

Source: *Business Week*, 1994.

But most troublesome is the very concept of "net taxes" as a measure of the net burden imposed by government, let alone of the relative welfare of generations. Suppose, as is likely, future generations are paying taxes to finance interest payments on the federal debt. To whom are those interest payments going? Only a small portion of the debt is held by foreigners. Will it not be those same future generations that are receiving the interest payments? Are not the interest receipts an offset to the taxes that finance them? If we are looking for a measure of the net burden imposed by government, do we not want a comprehensive measure of the net amounts government takes from the public and not, as Mr. Kotlikoff himself has described them, the

41

government's arbitrarily classified receipts and "benefits" or transfers?

Suppose further that we levy taxes on the old to pay for the education of the young, as in fact we do. Is that not a transfer to new and coming generations? Suppose the government spends for roads, bridges and airports or in support of research, public and private. Are those expenditures not creating benefits and income for future generations? Take even outlays for defense, which I find particularly excessive in this post–Cold War world. To the extent they are necessary, are not we of the present generation who pay for them providing benefits of security and freedom for those who come after us?

Of course, wasteful expenditures may provide no benefits to our children. But does even the most ardent opponent of "government spending" believe that it is all wasteful?

Debt as an Asset

In fact, neither the "debt" with which each infant is born nor the "net taxes" he can expect to pay tells us anything about how well off he will be in any absolute sense or compared with his parents. The government debt may be better viewed as an *asset* of the American public, its predominant owners. We might say that each infant born today is given a nest egg of government saving bonds, or Treasury bills, notes, and bonds equal to $50,000. Is that a burden? And the net taxes, even if correctly projected and calculated, tell us nothing about either the total net benefits the public will receive from its government or, more important, how well it will be living.

To get at that we need comprehensive measures of what we as a nation are saving and investing for the future. These have little directly to do with entitlements or government debt, deficits or net taxes. The new measures would count the construction of new housing and the level of investment in new plants, equipment, research and technology. These measures would include government investment in infrastructure and the vital, intangible capital of basic research, health, education and the provision of a safe, secure society. They would include all of the investment, public and private, in human capital, in the formation of new generations well-trained and well-equipped for productive jobs in a technologically advancing economy.

Deficit Folly

Unfortunately, much of the political posturing and paranoia about budget deficits and government debt, and now the dire numbers from the so-called generational accounts, lead us in a different direction. Money that might go to expanded and better health care, we are told by many in the Congress, must instead be used to reduce the deficit. Money to prevent crime, to get people from welfare to work, to salvage much of a generation growing up functionally illiterate and outside of the productive economy—all such spending must be curbed to hold down deficits or future net taxes.

Proper, comprehensive generational accounting might help protect us from such folly. What we have so far only compounds the confusion about the vital issue of providing for our future.

Periodical Bibliography

The following articles have been selected to supplement the diverse views presented in this chapter. Addresses are provided for periodicals not indexed in the *Readers' Guide to Periodical Literature*, the *Alternative Press Index*, or the *Social Sciences Index*.

Neal E. Cutler	"As Does Everything Else About Baby Boomers, Retirement Prospects Vary Markedly," *Perspective on Aging*, October–December 1994. Available from the National Council on the Aging, 409 Third St. SW, Washington, DC 20024.
Ken Dychtwald	"A Future Glimpse at Our Aging Society," *Washington Post National Weekly Edition* (advertising supplement), May 1–7, 1995. Available from Reprints, 1150 15th St. NW, Washington, DC 20071.
Christopher Farrell	"The Economics of Aging: Why the Growing Number of Elderly Won't Bankrupt America," *Business Week*, September 12, 1994.
Karen Foote	"The Aging Population," *Issues in Science and Technology*, Winter 1994/1995.
D.E. Herz	"Work After Early Retirement: An Increasing Trend Among Men," *Monthly Labor Review*, April 1995.
Stanley Jacobson	"Overselling Depression to the Old Folks," *Atlantic Monthly*, April 1995.
Robert Lewis	"Here Come the Boomers! Broad Social Effects Seen," *AARP Bulletin*, December 1995. Available from PO Box 199, Long Beach, CA 90801.
William S. Rukeyser	"Let's Do the Hobble," *Atlantic Monthly*, July 1995.
Michael Rust	"Disparate Interest Groups Vie for Hearts of Elderly," *Insight*, November 27, 1995. Available from 3600 New York Ave. NE, Washington, DC 20002.
USA Today	"Baby Boomers Threaten Entire Pension System," April 1995.
Arnold Wagner	"Second Childhood," *JAMA*, August 23–30, 1995. Available from AMA, 515 N. State St., Chicago, IL 60610.
Jacob Weisberg	"The Coming War Between the Old and the Young," *Worth*, June/July 1992. Available from 575 Lexington Ave., New York, NY 10022.

2 CHAPTER

Should Entitlement Programs for Seniors Be Reformed?

Chapter Preface

As warnings increase about an impending collapse of Social Security and Medicare, many experts are proposing measures to reform America's two largest entitlement programs. One approach favored by many policy analysts and others is to privatize both systems.

Under a privatized system of Social Security, workers would deposit mandatory contributions in accounts managed by private firms rather than pay taxes into the federal Social Security trust fund. If Medicare were privatized, eligible Americans could elect to use government vouchers to choose the most suitable of competing private health plans or opt for Medicare coverage.

Proponents argue that these reforms would lead to greater benefits and services for older Americans. As a successful model, they cite Chile's private social security system. There, according to radio commentator John Gizzi, workers' "pension funds, unlike Social Security in the United States, have continued to grow at an average 10 percent per annum." Similarly, reformers argue that under a privatized system of Medicare, Americans would be allowed to select the coverage that best suits their needs. Advocates contend that the increase in consumer choice and industry competition would result in older Americans' receiving better value and a higher quality of services.

But opponents respond that privatization would endanger the guaranteed benefits and services that Social Security and Medicare have provided to seniors for decades. People who support strengthening Social Security, such as American Association of Retired Persons executive director Horace Deets, argue that the government system is sound enough (through the year 2030) that it does not require such a drastic reform as privatization. Deets contends that privatized Social Security would fail to provide numerous guaranteed benefits, including cost-of-living adjustments, a greater return on low-wage earners' investments, and payments to deceased or disabled workers and their dependents.

Entitlements such as Social Security and Medicare are a prime concern to most older Americans and an important issue for younger citizens as well. The authors in the following chapter debate whether these entitlement programs should be reformed.

*"It is yet possible to deal with [Social Security]
without cutting benefits—providing we act soon."*

Social Security
Should Be Rescued

Alan Simpson

Alan Simpson is a Republican U.S. senator from Wyoming. In
the following viewpoint, Simpson argues that Social Security
should be rescued through reforms that would not cut recipients' benefits. Simpson proposes gradually increasing the normal retirement age and placing a ceiling on the amounts of cost-
of-living adjustments of Social Security benefits.

As you read, consider the following questions:

1. What action was taken in 1983 regarding Social Security,
   according to Simpson?
2. According to Simpson, how soon could the Social Security
   system become insolvent?
3. Which current group of Americans is unlikely to collect
   any Social Security benefits, in the author's opinion?

Alan Simpson, "The Social Security Pie: Save a Piece for the Kids," *Christian Science
Monitor*, March 10, 1995. Reprinted by permission of the author.

Even if Congress eliminated the entire federal discretionary budget outright—closed the schools and highways, dissolved the military, shut down the national parks and even Congress itself—the "automatic" increases in entitlements and payments on the national debt mean that mandatory spending would grow to exceed federal revenues by the year 2012.

This is *not* some paranoid fantasy. It is the inevitable result of trends certified by the Social Security and Medicare trustees themselves.

By the year 2030, according to their report, Social Security expenses will absorb 17 percent of the national payroll tax base, Medicare HI (health insurance) outlays another 8 percent, and Medicare SMI (supplemental health insurance) another 7 percent. Can you imagine an America in which 30 percent of its national payroll is necessary to support two programs, Social Security and Medicare, alone? If we continue to cry "hands off" of not only current benefits in these programs, but even the projected future *increases*, we will only plunge toward national insolvency—or minimum tax brackets of 40 percent and higher.

Even if we enacted a "perfect" health-care reform bill—and wipe out inflation in health care—the cost of health care would still absorb twice as much of the national economy in the year 2030 as it does today, simply because of the aging of the population.

When Social Security was enacted, there were more than ten Americans working to sustain each one who was collecting from the system. The average projected lifespan was then lower than the age of eligibility. Now there are roughly three workers left to support each collector of benefits and the average lifespan is approaching 78.

The past contributions of current retirees were long-ago insufficient to support the benefits that are being paid out, which is exactly why the system had to be saved from bankruptcy in 1983 with a massive tax hike on younger generations. The benefits that retirees currently receive bear no direct relationship to the sum of what they put in. They represent a transfer of money from the young to the old, regardless of wealth, plain and simple.

To best illustrate this, I include a statement of my own contributions to Social Security as well as my promised benefits. You will see that I stand to get back the entirety of my lifetime contributions in about three years.

Alan Simpson's Social Security Statement

YOUR EARNINGS RECORD

| | SOCIAL SECURITY | | |
YEARS	Maximum Taxable Earnings	Your Taxed Earnings	Estimated Taxes You Paid
1937–50	$ 3,000	$ 583	$ 5

48

1951	3,600	346	5
1952	3,600	0	0
1953	3,600	0	0
1954	3,600	0	0
1955	4,200	0	0
1956	4,200	0	0
1957	4,200	0	0
1958	4,200	0	0
1959	4,800	1,683	42
1960	4,800	4,800	216
1961	4,800	4,800	144
1962	4,800	4,800	225
1963	4,800	4,800	259
1964	4,800	4,800	174
1965	4,800	4,800	174
1966	6,600	6,600	382
1967	6,600	6,600	257
1968	7,800	7,800	452
1969	7,800	7,800	327
1970	7,800	7,800	491
1971	7,800	7,800	358
1972	9,000	9,000	414
1973	10,800	10,800	523
1974	13,200	13,200	653
1975	14,100	14,100	697
1976	15,300	15,300	757
1977	16,500	16,500	816
1978	17,700	17,700	1,256
1979	22,900	8,724	615
1980	25,900	13,501	951
1981	29,700	6,801	544
1982	32,400	17,652	1,420
1983	35,700	21,851	1,759
1984	37,800	37,800	2,041
1985	39,600	39,600	2,257
1986	42,000	42,000	2,394
1987	43,800	43,800	2,496
1988	45,000	45,000	2,727
1989	48,000	48,000	2,908
1990	51,300	51,300	3,180
1991	53,400	53,400	3,310
1992	55,500	55,500	3,441
1993	57,600	57,600	3,571
1994	60,600		

ESTIMATED BENEFITS

Retirement

You must have 40 Social Security credits to qualify for retirement benefits and also for Medicare at age 65. Assuming that you meet all the requirements, here are estimates of your retirement benefits based on your past and any projected earnings. The estimates are in today's dollars.

If you get benefits at 62, your reduced monthly
amount in today's dollars will be about ....$ 940

The earliest age at which you can get an unreduced
benefit is 65 years of age. We call this your full
retirement age. If you wait until that age to get benefits,
your monthly amount in today's dollars will be about ....$ 1,135

If you wait until you are age 70 to get benefits, your
monthly amount in today's dollars will be about ....$ 1,510

Source: Social Security Administration

Even if you include employer contributions and interest payments, someone contributing the maximum amount payable into Social Security during the years 1950 to 1993 makes a maximum total contribution during this period of $39,856.77, which with interest would equal approximately $109,315.22. This recipient stands to receive it all back in 7.9 years, meaning that he or she is likely to eventually collect it back nearly two times over—and that's including the employer contributions and interest. The situation with lower-income recipients is even more generous.

Too Valuable to Lose

"Will Social Security be there for me and mine in the future? We think the answer is assuredly, "Yes." While technical reasoning supports such a conclusion, the answer is perhaps most simply arrived at through political logic.

No matter what your view, a leap of faith is necessary. A negative answer assumes somewhere in the future that the political leadership of the United States will be willing to take the political risk of eliminating or dramatically scaling back Social Security protections, either because the economy of the future cannot sustain it or because the program lacks political support. An affirmative response assumes, whatever strains emerge, the continuity of an economy that can afford Social Security and the continuity of government and public support for the program.

Simply put, we believe that Social Security will continue, not only because the concept is fundamentally sound and the program's financing challenges are manageable, but also because it is too important an institution for Congress or any president to take the political risk of allowing it to go bankrupt.

Eric R. Kingson and Edward D. Berkowitz, *Social Security and Medicare: A Policy Primer*, 1993.

However, the picture changes dramatically for the younger generation. Not only are younger workers unlikely to ever live long enough to collect back the huge taxes they are paying for retirement benefits, but the entire system itself stands to be insolvent by the year 2029 (according to the system's own trustees)—or, as early as 2014, if the government does not balance its books.

The challenge of controlling government spending, therefore, amounts to the challenge of controlling automatic government spending, which goes out in the form of entitlement payments each year: Social Security, Medicare, Medicaid, and federal retirement. This spending amounted to only 29.6 percent of the budget in 1963. But it grew to 45 percent in 1973, 56.3 percent in 1983, 61.4 percent in 1993, and will increase to 72 percent in 2003 if no action is taken.

Proposed Reforms

I suggest we gradually phase in an upward shift in the normal retirement age, eventually reaching an age of 70 for those 28 and under. *No one currently over the age of 50 would be affected by this change.* Interestingly, this proposal meets with stern and often rabid opposition from various seniors' groups, but receives support from younger Americans. Small wonder—those currently 28 and under do not now stand to collect *anything* from Social Security, as it is headed for bankruptcy.

I also proposed reforms in the measurement of the Consumer Price Index to more accurately reflect inflation. The "market basket" that is employed to measure the rising cost of living is updated only each decade under current law. In an era of rapid change this results in a seriously inaccurate measure of what people must buy.

Finally, I proposed a ceiling on the amounts of cost-of-living adjustments (COLAs) given to retirees in Social Security (as well as congressional, military, and all other federal retirement). Too often a COLA does not represent a change in the "cost of living" so much as "the cost of living it up." I propose that "needy" recipients receive their full COLA as granted under current law, but that recipients with greater benefits receive COLAs that are no larger. COLAs were *never* an original feature of Social Security and so in *no way* affect the original Social Security "contract" with America's workers.

These are my solutions. They are not popular, but I propose them because I believe it is yet possible to deal with this situation without cutting benefits—providing we act soon. That situation will shortly change if we decide instead for inaction.

It's our choice. Either we face the reality that Social Security, Medicare, and Medicaid must be reformed, or we leave posterity holding the sack—and the bounced check for our excesses.

"Let's ditch the [Social Security] Trust Fund altogether."

Social Security Should Not Be Rescued

Richard Thau

According to its trustees, America's Social Security system will become insolvent by the year 2029. In the following viewpoint, Richard Thau argues that the Social Security system is a doomed program that unfairly taxes younger workers and that will fail to pay them necessary retirement benefits. Thau contends that workers' taxes will have to be raised substantially to sustain Social Security. The author instead proposes a phased-in, mandatory private retirement account system to replace Social Security and provide an economic boost to America and its workers. Thau is the executive director of Third Millennium, a New York City advocacy organization of post–baby boomers and others concerned with America's future.

As you read, consider the following questions:

1. Why will the American Association of Retired Persons have to change its position on Social Security, in Thau's opinion?
2. According to Thau, how would a privatized system benefit America's economy?
3. According to the author, what is Social Security projected to pay to a single male born in 1965, relative to what he contributed?

Excerpted from Richard Thau, "Social Security: Should the Sacred Cow Be Slaughtered?" a speech delivered at the Cato Institute, March 28, 1995. Reprinted by permission of the author.

Since we launched [Third Millennium] in 1993, we've focused quite heavily on debt and deficit issues. We've spoken out about the need to reform entitlements—in newspaper op-eds, on college campuses, via fee media, and in direct testimony before a half-dozen different Congressional committees. We're the group that commissioned the poll that found more people 18–34 believe in UFOs than in the future of Social Security. . . .

The dirty little secret that must be exposed is this: Social Security and Medicare are running out of money. The so-called Trust Funds—supposedly containing hundreds of billions of dollars saved for our future—are nothing more than treasure chests cynically filled with IOUs. And today's young people, and our children and grandchildren, will be stuck footing the bill for today's deception. *It is unconscionable and must stop.*

Social Security's Coming Crisis

You probably know what the year 2029 represents. It's the current estimate of when Social Security will become insolvent because the so-called Trust Fund officially will be empty. Just think of the irony: if we fail to act now, Americans in 2029 will probably be too busy dealing with their own Social Security crisis to mark the one hundredth anniversary of the 1929 stock market crash that hastened the birth of Social Security.

I doubt, though, that we will fail to wait until 2029, or even 2012, to deal with Social Security's funding crisis. And that's because once today's seniors pass from the scene, the emotional, nostalgic attachment between Social Security recipients and Uncle Sam will evaporate.

In March 1995, *USA Today* presented the results of a poll showing that 59 percent of Americans over 50 think that Social Security will be available when they retire. But only 18 percent of Baby Boomers and 32 percent of Xers [members of the following generation, known as Generation X] agree. And once these Boomers become members of AARP [American Association of Retired Persons], a process that began in 1995, an internal conflict between elderly and middle-aged members is destined to occur within America's largest lobby. And that conflict will blur AARP's position, weaken its hold on Congress, and enable politicians to act more responsibly.

Simply put, demographics will be destiny. People who are 50 today will be 67 when Social Security is projected to hit deficit spending in 2012. If nothing is done now, the so-called Trust Funds, being nothing more than a massive collection of paper promises, will be short on money to pay these just-retired Boomers their benefits. To raise the necessary funds, taxes on workers will have to be hiked drastically. Workers will balk.

In the face of this scenario, I am convinced it will become increasingly difficult for AARP to justify its "Social-Security-is-sacred-so-forget-affluence-testing" posture. [Affluence-testing is a system for determining benefits based on the recipient's income.] Millions of Boomers, skeptical of Social Security's ability to provide for everyone, will be lured into AARP's ranks each year. And fearing that Social Security will go bust when they need their money most, when they're in their 70s and 80s, Boomers will invariably agree to affluence-testing for Social Security in order to salvage the entire system. The AARP elders will finally have to bend.

A Complete Overhaul

In the meantime, my [post–Baby Boomer] generation, witnessing what is likely to become a very ugly battle between reform-minded 50-somethings and purist 70-somethings, will seek a complete overhaul of the nation's retirement system and pursue a mandatory private system similar to Chile's.

According to the national poll Third Millennium commissioned in September 1994, 82 percent of young Americans want to be given the freedom to invest all or part of their Social Security payments in private retirement accounts that they would own, control and even pass along to their children and grandchildren.

A privatized Social Security system, phased in over time, would institutionalize a tremendous boost in savings and capital formation. It would keep interest rates low and provide tens of billions of dollars to the economy that could be used for new plants and equipment, research and development and worthwhile investment projects. Think of the huge opportunity for economic growth we'll create if we responsibly invest our FICA [Federal Insurance Contributions Act] funds in mutual funds, stocks and bonds, for example. . . .

Let's ditch the Trust Fund altogether. Instead, let's require workers to put 15 percent of what they now pay into Social Security—the part of their contributions currently earmarked for the Trust Fund—into an IRA [individual retirement account] or 401(K) plan. No current Social Security recipient's benefits would be affected. But every worker paying into Social Security would suddenly know that approximately one-seventh of their current contributions would be working for them, not for Uncle Sam. . . .

[There] is a growing rift between the way my peers view Social Security vs. how today's seniors view it. For people of my grandparents' era, it was social insurance, a promise made by [U.S. president Franklin D. Roosevelt] to them, almost personally, to have Uncle Sam take care of them when they grew old. All they had to do was make a modest contribution with each paycheck.

For people in my generation, however, Social Security is *just another tax*—and a considerable one at that. In fact, the running joke is that people in their 20s graduate from school, find a job, and then get their first paycheck. Money is deducted by the Federal government, the state government and the city government. And then there's a big chunk forked over to FICA. And the question becomes: "Who is this FICA and why is he taking so much money from my paycheck?"

The Present Trend Is Not Sustainable

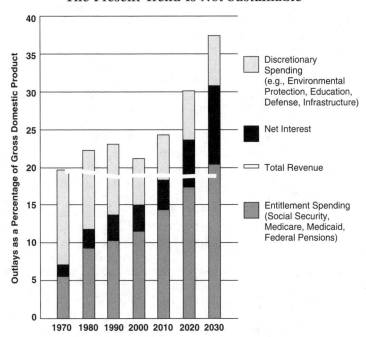

This chart shows how America will become bankrupt if we fail to control spending on entitlement programs, such as Social Security and Medicare. The white line hovering around 19 percent represents the federal government's revenues (as a percentage of the total U.S. economy). The vertical bars show how the Federal government has spent (and will spend) its revenues. All spending above the white line represents borrowing.

Source: Bipartisan Commission on Entitlement & Tax Reform, 1994.

This isn't just innocent ignorance. It's the failure of government to justify Social Security's existence to young workers who have no idea why 7.65 percent of their salaries are taken from them each week. And remember, for the self-employed, the

FICA figure doubles to 15.3 percent.

Put yourself in the position of a typical 22-year-old who might know a little more about FICA than, say, someone who thinks it's a person. You're watching the news one night and hear that the Social Security Trustees are projecting that insolvency is moving closer—that it's going to arrive before you retire because the Baby Boomers will exhaust the system. Is it natural to think you're being swindled? Of course.

And then you hear about plans to correct the problem. Certain people suggest raising Social Security taxes by one or two percentage points to get the system back into actuarial balance. Well, payroll taxes have multiplied ten times since 1950, from 3 percent on the first $3,000 earned to 12.4 percent on the first $61,200 earned. Adding the employer's and employee's FICA contributions, most young workers pay more in payroll taxes than in Federal taxes. Hiking payroll taxes quickly sounds like a lousy option. . . .

No More Transfers of Wealth

Let's recognize that Social Security, even if it were to survive past 2029, is projected to be a lousy investment for my generation. According to "Retooling Social Security for the 21st Century," published in 1994 by the Urban Institute, a single male born in 1915 with an average lifetime income received back $39,000 more than he paid into Social Security over his lifetime. That's in constant 1993 dollars with interest. A single male born the same year I was, in 1965, with an average lifetime income is projected to get back $46,000 less than he put in over his working life. And remember, this is the projection if Social Security somehow makes it past its insolvency date!

Starting with people of my generation, let's transition to a system of mandatory private retirement accounts where there's a chance for positive return. Given a choice of ten or twenty government-approved and regulated retirement plans, citizens could pick any one that caught their fancy. Novice investors could pick a basic combination fund that equally divided their retirement funds among all available plans. Contributions would be extracted just as they are now, from paychecks.

Imagine this: No more Trust Fund hoaxes, no more transfers of wealth from young to old and poor to rich. And no more presuming that Depression-era thinking should prevail forever.

"*Privatization of Social Security can restore financial dignity to Americans' retirement years.*"

Social Security Should Be Privatized

William G. Shipman

Anticipating a collapse of Social Security, some experts have proposed privatizing the system, allowing workers to contribute part of their wages to personal retirement accounts managed by financial institutions. In the following viewpoint, William G. Shipman argues that workers given the freedom to invest their wages would receive much higher returns than Social Security would provide. Shipman points to Chile as a nation that has successfully privatized its social security system. Shipman is cochairman of the Cato Institute's Project on Social Security Privatization and is a principal with State Street Global Advisors in Boston.

As you read, consider the following questions:

1. According to Shipman, what financial assets could workers invest in under a privatized system?
2. What would be the effect of some suggested Social Security reforms, in the author's opinion?
3. What are Chile's pension fund companies obligated to do, according to Shipman?

Excerpted from William G. Shipman, "Retiring with Dignity: Social Security vs. Private Markets," *Cato Project on Social Security Privatization*, no. 2, August 14, 1995. Reprinted by permission of the Cato Institute.

Retiring with financial dignity is in jeopardy. That is the direct result of Social Security's ever-expanding role in the economics of both retirees and workers. Compassionate in intent, but flawed in design, Social Security will prevent many from enjoying financial security in their later years.

Unlike personal savings, pensions, and independent retirement accounts, all of which are stores of wealth, Social Security is a misguided political construct, wherein one's retirement benefits are dependent on the willingness of future workers to be taxed.

Benefits paid to present recipients are low. Benefits to be paid to future recipients will be even lower. Worse, the legal requirement to pay Social Security taxes prevents workers from investing the money lost to those taxes in higher earning assets.

Beyond that, the unsound financial foundation of the system virtually ensures that the promised benefits, low as they are, will be reduced even further. In the past, when Social Security's financial precariousness was addressed, the legislative response was to increase taxes and reduce benefits. Such responses not only failed to solve the problem, they exacerbated it.

There is a better solution. Allow people the freedom to invest their Federal Insurance Contributions Act (FICA) taxes in financial assets such as stocks and bonds. History shows that the financial return on those instruments meets retirement needs at a fraction of Social Security's cost.

For example, assuming historical rates of return, if individuals born in 1970 were allowed to invest in stocks the amount they currently pay in Social Security taxes, those individuals could receive nearly six times the benefits that they are scheduled to receive under Social Security, as much as $11,729 per month. Even a low-wage earner would receive nearly three times the return on Social Security.

The idea of privatizing a public pension system is neither new nor untried. Where it has been properly implemented, it has been remarkably successful. For governments, privatization is the only viable answer to Social Security's inherent problems; for individuals, it is a profitable one. . . .

Workers Bear the Burden

Workers are required by law to pay Social Security taxes. That precludes their investing those lost wages in higher yielding assets such as those held in their personal savings and pension plans. They incur a huge burden from that loss of freedom because Social Security is a tremendously bad investment.

How bad depends on several factors such as date of birth, age at retirement, investment alternatives, and lifetime income. The following analysis looks at pairs of workers born in 1930, 1950, and 1970. One of each pair's income is low—50 percent of the national average wage. The other's income is high—Social Security's maximum covered earnings. To put that in some perspective, in 1995 those wages were about $12,600 and $61,200, respectively. Each worker is assumed to start employment at age 21 and retire at either age 62 or the normal retirement age of 65, 66, or 67 depending on date of birth. Investment choices are restricted to U.S. stocks and bonds. Stocks are a 75/25 percent mix of large and small capitalization companies. Bonds are a 50/50 percent mix of long-term corporate and government bonds. Stock and bond returns are those actually earned from 1951 to 1993. Nominal returns thereafter are assumed to be 7

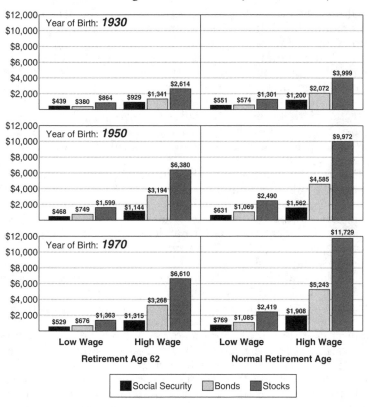

Figure 1. Monthly Benefit Comparison of Social Security and the Capital Markets by Date of Birth, Income, and Age of Retirement (1995 Dollars)

Source: William G. Shipman.

and 10 percent for bonds and stocks, respectively. At retirement, portfolios are used to purchase annuities, increasing at 4 percent per annum and certain to age 80. Figure 1 compares Social Security's benefits to those earned from the capital markets for each of the cohorts.

The results are a striking indictment of Social Security. In every case but one, Social Security's benefits are below those earned in the capital markets. That phenomenon is not new. Both workers and retirees have been disadvantaged for decades. What the public has been encouraged to think is a secure, funded, government pension program that offers retirees reasonable benefits in return for taxes on their labor is, in fact, something else. It is a coercive, intergenerational transfer tax system that relies on unrealistic assumptions and pays unreasonably low benefits. . . .

Social Security Cannot Be Fixed

Ultimately, even if Social Security's looming financial difficulties can be fixed, it remains a fundamentally flawed program, providing an increasingly bad deal for today's young workers. Indeed, the reforms suggested for restoring the trust fund's actuarial balance, such as increasing payroll taxes, raising the retirement age, and reducing COLAs [cost-of-living adjustments], would actually reduce the relative rate of return.

It, therefore, becomes imperative to move quickly to a private pension system. Where privatization has been effectively implemented, it has been successful. The Chilean experience is instructive.

Only a brief comment will be offered about the Chilean system, for a full and detailed explanation is beyond the scope of this viewpoint. Also, the Chilean model may not be precisely applicable to the United States. That said, however, Chile confronted a substantially similar problem with its public pension system and privatized it. The new private system has been remarkably successful.

Chile's social security system predated ours, having started in 1926. In the late 1970s its benefit payments were greater than its taxes, and it had no funded reserves. The anticipated decline in its support/benefit ratio meant that the problems were only going to get worse. Chile decided to fundamentally restructure its system, not merely reform the flawed pay-as-you-go scheme.

The new system is one of forced savings. Workers are required to contribute 10 percent of their wages to their own accounts at a pension fund company (Administradoras de Fondos de Pensiones, or AFP), which invests the wages in securities such as stocks and bonds. Contributions and investment returns are not taxed, but withdrawals are. At retirement, participants have the options of purchasing a life-long annuity, withdrawing a monthly benefit from their AFP account, or purchasing an annuity that is effective at a specified future date. Participants also have the right to contribute an additional 10 percent of after-tax wages to their accounts, which compound tax-free.

Generous Pensions

A privately managed retirement system may seem wholly impractical and out of touch with political reality. But this is precisely what Chile has been doing for 13 years, since people there became fed up with the public system. Several private funds actively compete in Chile for the right to manage the savings that workers are required to put aside for their old age. Government regulations require private management funds to have minimum capitalization, and they limit investments to particular categories of securities.

Although expenses were high during the early years in Chile, they have fallen sharply over time as experience with the system has grown. The inflation-adjusted annual rate of return on investments from 1981 to 1990 was more than 12%. And the pensions awarded so far under this system have been generous compared with those offered by the old system.

Gary S. Becker and Isaac Ehrlich, *Wall Street Journal*, March 30, 1994.

The AFPs are single-purpose companies that are licensed and regulated by the government. Among other obligations, they are required to invest the contributions, distribute the benefits, offer insurance, conduct participant record keeping, and keep a certain level of reserves. Much as they are in our mutual fund industry, the workers' assets are separate from the AFP's assets. If an AFP were to go out of business, participants' assets would be transferred to another AFP. Individuals have the right to choose and change their AFP.

Greater Savings and Benefits

The success of Chile's privatization of its public pension system can be measured in many ways. Whereas in the late 1970s there were virtually no savings, now the cumulative assets managed by AFPs are about $23 billion, or roughly 41 percent of gross domestic product [GDP]. During the past decade, growth of Chile's real GDP has averaged over 6 percent, more than double that of the United States. And for the five years ending in 1994, the annualized total return of the Chilean stock market was 48.6 percent versus 8.7 percent for the United States.

But most important, retirees are receiving much higher benefits. Since the privatized system became fully operational on May 1, 1981, the average rate of return on investment has been 14 percent per year. As a result, the typical retiree is receiving a benefit equal to nearly 80 percent of his average annual income over the last ten years of his working life, almost double the U.S. replacement value.

Chile's reforms are seen as such a huge economic and political success that other Latin American countries, including Argentina, Peru, and Colombia, are beginning to implement similar changes. Mexico has implemented a new privatized social security system operating alongside its old state-run system. In Europe, Britain has allowed some people to opt out of its upper tier of benefits, and Italy has begun to privatize some aspects of its social security system. Several former Soviet bloc countries also are studying the issue, for their systems are in precarious financial condition.

The U.S. Social Security system is not as vulnerable today as some others were when they were privatized. That gives us a window of opportunity within which to move forward with a reasoned solution without being subject to imminent crisis during the planning. But move forward we must, for the future of our system, if not changed, is certain disaster. We can do better for our younger workers and older retirees than to wait for the inevitable.

Allowing individuals to invest their money directly in the capital markets, rather than in Social Security, will provide them with far higher returns and thereby greater financial security. Thus, privatization of Social Security can restore financial dignity to Americans' retirement years.

"Privatization . . . would destroy a system that has worked well for decades."

Social Security Should Not Be Privatized

Horace Deets

Horace Deets is the executive director of the American Association of Retired Persons (AARP), an advocacy and lobbying organization with more than thirty million members over age fifty. In the following viewpoint, Deets asserts that Social Security is a successful program that should be strengthened, not privatized. Deets contends that privatization of the system would be ineffective because many Americans would not independently contribute to their personal retirement accounts. He maintains that a privatized system would be too economically risky, leaving millions of Americans unprotected and paying less income to recipients than the current system.

As you read, consider the following questions:

1. In Deets's opinion, what impact does Social Security have on the federal deficit?
2. Who is protected by Social Security's progressive-benefits formula, according to Deets?
3. What examples of investment catastrophes does the author give?

Horace Deets, "No: Cost and Risk Are Prohibitive"; author's response to question: Could Privatization Avert a Social Security Crisis? posed in the May 29, 1995, *Insight* magazine. Reprinted with permission of *Insight*. Copyright 1993 by The Washington Times Corporation. All rights reserved.

"I cannot too strongly urge the wisdom of building upon the principles contained in the present Social Security Act in affording greater protection to our people, rather than turning to untried and demonstrably unsound panaceas," President Franklin D. Roosevelt told Congress in his message recommending improvements in the Social Security system in 1939. His words easily could apply to the debate today over the privatization of Social Security.

Privatization—a proposal to replace the Social Security system with private retirement accounts—is just such "an unsound panacea." At first blush, privatization sounds like a good idea; after all, people should take responsibility to plan for their retirement. However, when it comes time to retire they may find that they receive even less income from their privatized personal retirement account than they would have received from Social Security.

Social Security Works Well

Proponents of the privatization of Social Security claim that Social Security isn't working and ought to be replaced. They believe that Social Security's current structure, combined with the aging of the baby boomers, will lead the system into bankruptcy.

Yet, Social Security has worked well for sixty years, and there is no reason to believe that it is on the verge of bankruptcy. The truth is that the Social Security Old Age, Survivor and Disability Insurance, or OASDI, Trust Funds are adequately financed for the next twenty to twenty-five years and can continue to pay benefits without any change in the current law through 2030.

This is not to suggest that we should ignore Social Security's long-term solvency needs. In fact, we should begin discussing the moderate reforms that will be required to keep the program sound for future generations.

Privatization, however, should not be part of the debate because it would destroy a system that has worked well for decades and would force older Americans, survivors and disabled persons in future generations to live in poverty.

In the thirties, Roosevelt saw Social Security as the basis "for the kind of protection America wants" from the financial burdens of old age and family tragedies. Today, Social Security provides economic security to forty-four million beneficiaries, including more than three million children under the age of 18, and about four million disabled workers under 65.

And that doesn't even count the indirect benefits that young families receive to protect them from the often extensive cost and responsibility of caring for older or disabled relatives. Today, 13 percent of older Americans live below the poverty line. Yet, without Social Security, half of our nation's older people would be poor.

The fact is, at a time when many government programs are criticized as being inefficient, bureaucratic and even unnecessary, Social Security continues to work efficiently and effectively as a family protection program. And, it also works economically and financially.

With a reserve in the OASDI Trust Funds approaching $500 billion, Social Security is self-funded and does not contribute to the federal deficit. If anything, it makes the deficit appear smaller because of its offsetting surplus. Moreover, the system is highly efficient, operating on an administrative overhead of 1 percent.

Social Security's Concepts

The success of Social Security is reflective of the support it receives from Americans of all ages. They support it because it is based on a set of concepts that have stood the test of time.

• The system is universal. Except for some state, local and federal government employees, virtually all working Americans and their employers contribute to the system. This means the OASDI Trust Funds are big enough to provide benefits regardless of risk or income level.

• The benefits are earned. Social Security is a contributory system. If you contribute during your working life, you and your family will be protected.

• The benefits are portable and inflation-proof. No matter where you work or how many times you change jobs, you continue to build credit toward Social Security benefits. And the benefits are adjusted annually to keep pace with the cost of living—a protection that is not provided by other pensions or annuities.

• Upon death, your spouse and eligible dependents receive benefits. The OASDI Trust Funds pay benefits to dependents and survivors of insured workers, benefits that could be equivalent to a $300,000 life-insurance policy. Spouses of deceased insured workers receive partial benefits before they reach 65 and full benefits if they wait until 65.

• If you become disabled, you and your dependents can receive benefits, even if you have not reached retirement age. If you have children under 18, the family's benefits are increased.

These concepts would be destroyed if Social Security were privatized. A privatized system would not necessarily be universal because many people simply would not save on their own. To work effectively, the government would have to be involved, forcing people to save. That means government would be put in the position of placing restrictions on the withdrawal and use of the savings and mandating how much people have to save.

Furthermore, personal retirement accounts would not work for most people. For example, they would not work for part-time or temporary workers—who are becoming more prevalent in the American economy. And, they would not work for low-wage earners.

The Harms of a Privatized System

The current system is structured progressively so that lower-wage earners receive more in benefits than they pay into the system. Additionally, Social Security recipients who earn more than $34,000 ($44,000 as a couple) are taxed on as much as 85 percent of their benefits—essentially all but what they contributed while working. This progressive-benefits formula helps keep fifteen million people of all ages out of poverty. A privatized system removes the progressive-benefits formula that helps low-wage earners get a larger return on their investment. They would suffer from a privatized system, and many would be forced to live out their lives in poverty. The current Social Security system protects these people through its progressive-benefits formula.

Prohibitive Costs

The costs of moving to a private retirement system are prohibitive. If younger workers were allowed to drop out of Social Security today, revenues to pay the benefits of Americans who have already retired or will leave the work force in the next few years would be reduced. The Social Security Administration estimates that Washington would have to come up with a staggering $8 trillion in new revenues to tide the system over until personal retirement accounts take over in the twenty-first century.

David Hage, *U.S. News & World Report*, April 3, 1995.

Under a private system, the risk of planning and investment would shift to the individual, rather than the shared, or pooled, risk under the social insurance system. As such, the investment no longer would be inflation-proof. Private investments simply do not provide cost-of-living adjustments. The size of your retirement nest egg would depend upon your skill as an investor. As shown by the investment catastrophes of the Orange County, California, government (which declared itself bankrupt in 1994 because of bad pension-fund investments) and Britain's Barings PLC bank (which was brought down in 1995 by the poor and risky investments of one manager), private investor success may be uncertain. In the end, taxpayers would be called upon to bail out those who didn't save for their retirement or who made bad investments. The current Social Security system spreads the investment risk, providing a more predictable retirement income.

Also, under a private system, those who became disabled—especially at a young age—would not have built a large-enough investment account to carry them through their lives with a decent standard of living. Likewise, they would have to rely even more on their skills as investors. And the inflation rate—especially health-care inflation, which continues to require people of all ages to pay more of their health-care costs from their own pockets—would eat away at their investment principal at an increasingly rapid pace.

Those favoring privatization of the Social Security system often fail to consider the cost of moving to a private retirement system. Current workers would have to pay for current beneficiaries as well as their own benefits. Otherwise, if younger workers were allowed to drop out of the Social Security system today, the money available to pay the benefits of those who are retired, or about to retire, would be reduced significantly. According to the Social Security Administration, workers would have to come up with $8 trillion in new revenue just to carry the system over until the personal retirement accounts would take effect in the twenty-first century. This fact, in itself, makes the privatization of Social Security economically prohibitive.

Strengthen Social Security

Privatizing Social Security is not the way to provide economic security for today's or future generations of retirees, survivors and disabled Americans. The best way to provide economic security is to strengthen Social Security, the private pension system and individual saving and investment.

Most people who will be retiring in the next fifteen to twenty years look to Social Security as a major source of retirement income. Why? Because they haven't been able to save and invest enough on their own, and because many will not have a pension and others will get only a modest pension. And they also are counting on it because they know Social Security does work—and we must see that it keeps on working.

Roosevelt was right. We must build on the principles upon which Social Security is based to offer even greater protection to the people. Now is not the time to turn to "untried and demonstrably unsound panaceas." If we endorse these untried and unsound panaceas—of which privatization certainly must be included—we run the risk of destroying Social Security and ending up with a nation where growing old means living a life of poverty. None of us wants that, especially when we realize that those people who would experience such hardship in their old age are our children and grandchildren.

"A new Medicare system based on consumer choice and competition . . . will mean health care choice and security for today's elderly."

Medicare Reform Will Benefit Seniors

Stuart M. Butler, Robert E. Moffit, and John C. Liu

Medicare is a federal health insurance program available primarily to Americans aged sixty-five years or older. In the following viewpoint, Stuart M. Butler, Robert E. Moffit, and John C. Liu contend that Medicare and its out-of-control costs must be replaced with a system that gives consumers a choice among competing health plans with varied benefits. The authors propose the nine-million-member Federal Employees Health Benefits Plan (FEHBP) as a model for Medicare reform. Butler and Moffit are policy directors, and John C. Liu is a policy analyst, for the Heritage Foundation, a conservative think tank in Washington, D.C.

As you read, consider the following questions:

1. What two choices does Congress have regarding Medicare's future, in the authors' opinion?
2. According to the authors, what is a defined contribution program?
3. What is responsible for FEHBP's controlled costs, according to the authors?

Excerpted from Stuart M. Butler, Robert E. Moffit, and John C. Liu, "What to Do About Medicare," *Heritage Foundation Backgrounder*, no. 1038, June 26, 1995. Reprinted by permission of the Heritage Foundation.

Designed to operate as a federally run health insurance program for America's elderly, Medicare was heralded by proponents as both "historic" and "fiscally responsible." Now, however, Medicare is essentially bankrupt, and its ability to maintain the quality of its services is in doubt. According to the 1995 Trustees Report, if Medicare is not reformed the cash flow of the HI trust fund (Part A), which finances hospital benefits for the elderly, will go into the red in fiscal year 1997 and the fund will run out of money and become insolvent in the year 2002. The report provides some sobering information on how payroll taxes (which finance the HI program) would have to rise to keep the program afloat without reform. "To bring the HI program into actuarial balance even for the first 25 years," reported the trustees, a new 1.3 percent payroll tax would have to be added on top of the current 2.9 percent Medicare payroll tax. Based on the trustees' estimates for revenues under the current tax rate, this would raise payroll taxes—and hence the cost of employing Americans—by an estimated $263 billion over five years and $388 billion over seven years. A worker earning $45,000 would have to pay an additional payroll tax of $292.50 per year.

An Increased Tax Burden

To achieve long-term actuarial balance of the HI trust fund without reforming the program—that is, to put it on a *permanently* sound footing—an immediate additional payroll tax of 3.52 percent would need to be levied on top of today's 2.9 percent rate. That would raise taxes by $711 billion over five years and $1.050 trillion over seven years. The payroll taxes of a worker earning $45,000 would increase by $1,584 per year.

And this is only to bail out the hospital program and enable those benefits to be paid. Part B [Medicare's voluntary monthly premium program] also will require a rapidly increasing subsidy from general revenues to continue paying for physician services. "Growth rates have been so rapid," explain the trustees, "that outlays of the program have increased 53 percent in aggregate and 40 percent per enrollee in the last five years. For the same period, the program grew 19 percent faster than the economy despite recent efforts to control the cost of the program." With the trustees' "intermediate" estimates of future program growth, the annual taxpayer subsidy will grow from an estimated $38 billion in fiscal year 1995 to an estimated $89 billion in 2000 and $147 billion in FY 2004.

Trying to hold down Medicare's costs through price controls on health providers and through stringent regulations is no answer. Not only has this strategy failed to control costs, it encourages physicians and hospitals to "game" the government rather than properly serve their patients. Moreover, price controls have shifted costs to the private sector, driving up premiums for working individuals and families.

Instead of trying to tighten current controls and regulations, the proper reform is to create a very different dynamic and set of incentives to drive the Medicare program. Specifically, the bureaucratic, standardized, command-and-control structure of today's Medicare must be replaced with consumer choice among competing plans offering different benefits. This is the same dynamic that has allowed health costs to be brought under control while improving quality in the private sector—and in the government-sponsored health plan enjoyed by Members of Congress and other federal employees.

Ability to Choose

The way to achieve the same results in Medicare is to pattern it broadly after the existing Federal Employees Health Benefits Plan (FEHBP), which covers almost nine million federal employees, families, and retirees, including present and former Members of Congress. This new program, perhaps renamed "Medi-Choice," would replace today's *defined benefit* program with a *defined contribution* program that gives America's seniors an unprecedented opportunity to choose their own health plan and range of benefits, just as retired Members of Congress and other federal retirees do. Under such a system, unlike today's Medicare program, the nation's elderly and disabled could choose sound health insurance from a variety of managed care and fee-for-service arrangements. And retirees could choose coverage for services not covered by today's standardized Medicare program—such as a prescription drug benefit—by accepting, say, higher copayments for other covered services. One of the great ironies of the Medicare debate is that those who oppose reform are denying the elderly the chance to receive many basic medical services already available to working Americans, and even to the indigent.

The key financial difference is that the government would make a defined financial contribution to the plan of the retiree's choice, rather than reimburse each Washington-approved service according to a fee schedule that defies comprehension and ignores market realities. This incentive encourages beneficiaries to pick plans with the best value for money, pocketing part of the savings from choosing more efficient coverage. It already has enabled spending in the FEHBP to increase at half the rate of Medicare, in addition to which federal workers and retirees in 1995 were treated to premium reductions averaging 3.3 percent. Introducing the same incentive system into a reformed Medicare program would save hundreds of billions of dollars, putting the program on a sound financial footing so that it can serve both today's elderly and the next generation of Americans.

Congress in reality has only two choices when considering the future of Medicare. One choice is to make no significant change in how Medicare is run and try to pay for future trust fund shortfalls either by raising payroll and other taxes or by diverting money from other programs. This means Medicare survives only by draining money from the rest of the budget or by raising taxes dramatically.

The second choice is to change the way Medicare is run so that benefits are delivered more efficiently, avoiding future tax increases or a diversion of money from other programs. Making the program more efficient not only will reduce the financial burden Medicare places on the next generation, but also will improve the quality of benefits and choices available to America's senior citizens. . . .

A Model for Reform—the FEHBP

Members of Congress searching for an alternative model for Medicare reform do not have to look far. For well over three decades, Members of Congress and federal employees—and federal retirees—have been enrolled in a unique consumer-driven health care system called the Federal Employees Health Benefits Program (FEHBP). Unlike Medicare, it is not run on the principles of central planning and price controls. Instead, it is based on the market principles of consumer choice and competition. Beginning in 1960 with fifty-one plans for the federal workforce, the FEHBP now encompasses over four hundred private health insurance plans nationwide, ranging from traditional indemnity insurance and fee-for-service to plans sponsored by federal unions and employee organizations to different forms of managed care, including health maintenance organizations (HMOs) and preferred provider organizations (PPOs). In the Washington, D.C., metropolitan area, half of all persons with health insurance are covered by one of the thirty-five plans competing in the FEHBP.

The FEHBP is entirely different from Medicare. For one thing, Medicare is a *defined benefit* program, meaning each enrollee has access to a specific set of health services which are paid for, in total or in part, by the federal government. The FEHBP, on the other hand, is a *defined contribution* program in which the government agrees to provide federal workers or retirees with a financial contribution they can use to purchase the health coverage of their choice.

Even more important, and unlike Medicare, the FEHBP does not attempt to constrain costs by controlling prices and specifying a comprehensive set of services. It sets only minimal guidelines over how plans must be structured and marketed. The law specifies only a brief category of core benefits, permitting federal workers and retirees to choose the plans and benefits that are right for them. Cost restraint is achieved not with an army of Medicare-style price controllers, but through the operation of consumer choice in a market of competing plans. That is why FEHBP spending is projected to increase at about 6 percent per year while spending for Medicare is expected to grow at 10 percent per year. . . .

Like Congressional Retirees

Congress should treat the elderly like congressional retirees and make available to citizen retirees a degree of choice equal to or superior to the level of choice available to retired Members of Congress and their spouses. Moreover, Congress should introduce improvements in the design of a consumer choice system in Medicare that would lessen the problems of adverse selection and forestall the kind of government regulatory interference which frustrates consumer choice and competition in the FEHBP.

Brenda Fitzgerald, *Heritage Foundation Backgrounder*, no. 1059, October 30, 1995.

The FEHBP is very popular among federal retirees—so popular that a significant number of federal retirees who enroll in Medicare keep their existing federal coverage as a "wraparound" plan. While Medicare is their primary source of insurance, the additional benefits included in the FEHBP (such as prescription drugs, catastrophic coverage, and preventive care) serve as more than adequate protection. As the National Association of Retired Federal Employees states in its 1995 guide to federal health plans for retirees, "All FEHB plans are good. . . . You can't make a serious mistake in choosing a FEHB plan unless you choose a high cost plan or option when you don't need one."

Federal retirees do not have merely a choice of plan. Unlike virtually all other Americans, active or retired, congressional and federal retirees also have the freedom to choose the services they want. Unlike Americans enrolled in Medicare, they are not locked into a single, government-standardized benefits package. Beyond the normal range of typical hospitalization and physician services, they can pick from a variety of plans that cover such items as skilled nursing care and home health care by a nurse, dental care, outpatient mental benefits, routine physical examinations, durable medical equipment and prostheses, hospice care, chemotherapy, radiation, physical and rehabilitative therapy, prescription drugs, mail order drugs, diabetic supplies, treatments for alcoholism or drug abuse, acupuncture, and chiropractic services. And FEHBP plans include catastrophic coverage—in sharp contrast to Medicare. . . .

A Reform Agenda for Medicare

Congress has committed itself to curbing the growth of Medicare spending in order to restore financial stability and prevent out-of-control spending from draining money from other programs or forcing huge increases in taxes. To carry out this wise commitment, Congress can proceed in two ways. It can impose tighter regulation and stricter price controls while cutting medical services for the elderly, as it has in the past. But experience shows that this strategy yields only short-term spending reductions at best. In the long run, it does nothing to curb runaway spending and undermines the quality of care for the elderly.

The other option for Congress is to achieve spending restraint by giving the elderly greater control over their Medicare dollars and greater opportunity to use their dollars to select the health care plans and services that are right for them. Such a reform, modeled after the system serving federal retirees, would use consumer choice and competition to curb waste and improve care.

Such a reform would include three principles:

Principle #1: Medicare should be changed from a defined benefit program to a defined contribution program.

Principle #2: The elderly should be allowed to use their Medicare dollars to enroll in a plan with health services that they choose, not services that bureaucrats or politicians have chosen for them.

Principle #3: Cost control should be achieved through consumer choice and competition, not central planning and price controls. HCFA's [Health Care Financing Administration] complex system of price controls and other restrictions should be phased out. . . .

Advantages of the Reform

A reform based on this consumer-choice approach would have numerous advantages for the elderly and the taxpayer.

• *Freedom to Choose Plans and Benefits.* Under a consumer choice Medicare system, elderly Americans could choose the private health insurance that best meets their individual needs. With the advice and counsel of their doctors, they could pick not only the level of benefits above a basic set of hospital and physician services, but also a broad range of medical services and treatments available on the free market—for instance, a plan with drug coverage or dental care—which they do not get under Medicare. Consulting with their doctors, rather than waiting for approval from HCFA bureaucrats, also means the elderly could take advantage of changes in treatments, medical procedures, and service delivery innovations—something lacking in today's Medicare. The only large elderly group with access to similar breakthroughs today are retired Members of Congress and federal employees.

• *Value for Money.* Like federal and congressional retirees, Medicare beneficiaries would be able to pocket any savings from their personal decisions. While the cost of health care is considerably higher for the elderly than for active workers and their families, the government contribution to their health plans also would be higher, depending on differences in age, sex, and geography.

• *Controlling Costs.* While by no means a perfect market, the FEHBP has been able to control costs better than either private, employer-based insurance or the current Medicare program, according to the Congressional Budget Office and such private econometric firms as Lewin-ICF. . . . In recent years, even though the FEHBP enrolls approximately 1.6 million higher-cost retirees and dependents and includes progressively higher benefits, outlays have increased at a much slower rate than the Medicare program's. With the establishment of a Medi-Choice system similar in structure to the current FEHBP, the powerful market forces of consumer choice and competition should produce similar dynamics and results in the Medicare program. . . .

Fundamental Restructuring

It is imperative that participants in this debate, particularly Members of Congress, focus their attention not only on the financial health, but also on the administrative structure, including the regulatory details, of the Medicare system. While pursuing necessary spending restraints in Medicare and other government programs in order to secure an end to ruinous deficits, lawmakers also must begin a fundamental restructuring of the program with a view toward improving the quality, availability, and security of health services for the elderly well into the twenty-first century.

If Congress fails to institute fundamental reform, either the elderly will be faced with a dramatic reduction in the quantity and the quality of their health care coverage, or already overburdened working families will be forced to pay sharply higher payroll taxes just to maintain the current level of benefits. Either consequence is tantamount to fiscal and political disaster. But if Congress uses this historic opportunity to create a new Medicare system based on consumer choice and competition, it will mean health care choice and security for today's elderly and a strong and solvent retirement health care system for future generations of Americans as well.

"It is with my Aunt May and Uncle Bernard in mind that I warily monitor congressional proposals to cut Medicare . . . funding."

Medicare Reform May Harm Seniors

Karen Houppert

Legislation to reform Medicare would threaten seniors' economic and physical well-being and do nothing to address the high costs of health care, Karen Houppert argues in the following viewpoint. Houppert opposes congressional efforts to slash the Medicare budget and create free-market voucher programs. She contends that such programs would require older Americans to make complicated decisions about health plans and would encourage for-profit health groups not to enroll at-risk seniors. Houppert is a staff writer for the *Village Voice* weekly newspaper.

As you read, consider the following questions:

1. According to Jim McDermott, cited by Houppert, why do Republicans need billions of dollars in Medicare cuts?
2. What risk assessment would seniors have to make under a voucher system of health care, in Houppert's opinion?
3. In the author's opinion, how would the monetary value of vouchers erode over time?

Excerpted from Karen Houppert, "Aging in America," *Village Voice*, September 19, 1995. Reprinted by permission of the author.

It is 10 p.m., and a shaft of light from the TV and the red glow of a blinking monitor are all that illuminate my Uncle Bernard. Once six feet two inches and 180 pounds, he now weighs a mere 95. His bony, bare legs angle out from under the covers and are no wider than my wrist. Most of his teeth have fallen out, his face is gaunt, his body still.

The week before, during physical therapy, a nurse broke his leg. His bones are fragile, disintegrating. But the therapy, which improves circulation, is supposed to help the bed sores that have begun to consume his body. After surgery to repair his leg, he had a stroke that left him partially paralyzed. He can barely move his throat to swallow or eat. He has bladder cancer. He has had multiple blood transfusions. He is senile.

When asked how he is feeling tonight, he complains of a headache. He mouths that he would very much like an aspirin.

My Aunt May stands next to her 90-year-old husband smoothing over a bandage that holds the IV in place on his forearm. . . .

Concern over Medicare Cuts

It is with my Aunt May and Uncle Bernard (May and Bernard are pseudonyms) in mind that I warily monitor congressional proposals to cut Medicare and Medicaid [a national health care program for the poor] funding.

Concern seems justified. In June 1995, Congress announced plans to cut $270 billion from Medicare and $182 billion from Medicaid; by September, it still hadn't announced just how it would do that. Viewed through the prism of my aunt and uncle's chaotic world, where myriad programs and services cobbled together over the years have sustained them, I have a million questions that quickie sound bites promising to "preserve, protect and strengthen Medicare" do not answer. I want to know: Will the elderly find their deductibles and copayments rising faster than their fixed incomes? Will, as President Bill Clinton predicts, thousands of elderly be squeezed out of the program altogether? Will Medicaid stop paying for nursing homes—like my uncle's—where annual costs range from $20,000 to $60,000? Will the visiting nurses who allow the infirm—like my aunt—to remain in their homes longer than they might otherwise still be covered under Medicare? If Medicaid shifts from an entitlement program, where everyone who qualifies can get insurance, to a block grant, where the states are given a finite amount to dole out as they see fit, what happens when the money for health care runs out? If the federal government, promising flexibility, hands over a Medicaid block grant, will it also relinquish its regulatory role—including such "interventions" as the protective legislation that monitors safety, comfort, and patient rights in nursing homes? Will the push for managed care sacrifice quality on the altar of expedience? Will a free-market approach to health care work for seniors? Has it worked for the rest of the country? Who wins with this legislation? Who loses? . . .

What began as a critique of the country's entire health care system has boiled down to an attack on Medicare (which, aside from the military, gets closest to a socialist model of care). Medicare has failed—and this is an assumption made across the board, by Democrats and Republicans alike—because it costs too much. Why? Because the elderly have not been frugal enough about going to the doctor. . . .

The Republican Scheme

According to drafts of the GOP [Grand Old Party; Republican] plan that were leaked to the *New York Times*, all the proposals under consideration take as their starting place the notion that seniors have not acted as cost-conscious consumers. From the voucher program that would propel the elderly into managed care to the medical savings accounts that would let them gamble on their own health to the higher copayments that would curb excessive use of doctors by making seniors feel the pinch in their pocketbook—these programs are designed to let the marketplace work its magic. And while many Democrats voice opposition to the GOP scheme, they are only objecting to the scale of the cuts, not their nature. . . .

Hoping to quell seniors' fears, Congress members and even President Clinton, who has jumped in with his own proposal to cut Medicare by $124 billion, carefully referred to the cuts as "reforms." The only articulate Democratic counterattack juxtaposes the $270 billion in Medicare cuts against the $245 billion in tax cuts. "The Republicans want you to believe that they are being forced to make drastic cuts in your Medicare benefits because the system is about to collapse," says Congress member Jim McDermott (Democrat, Washington). "[But] the Republican Medicare cuts have nothing whatsoever to do with saving the Medicare trust fund." He drives this home again and again: "Republicans need to cut $270 billion out of Medicare so that they can pay for their tax cuts to the well-off.". . .

Many Americans Will Be Affected

The GOP must convince the public that this legislation affects only the most marginal among us (the poor, the sick, the disabled, the "other"). But such arguments defy logic. Surely younger people in families beside my own—where it's obvious how precarious the support network is for our elderly, and obvious who will pick up the slack if things fall apart—spot holes in their reasoning. Such legislation will touch a lot of lives: seniors, of course (the 37 million Americans over 65); seniors-in-waiting (the 76 million baby boomers, who are next in line for benefits); the extended families that care for and about such seniors (the nation's twenty- and thirtysomethings); the neighbors and friends and extended families of the elderly (all those who offer to pick something up at the grocery store for grandma, to drop her by the doctor's office, to bring her dinner, or do her taxes); the unemployed and part-time workers (those 7.4 million adults who have no insurance other than Medicaid); the children of such adults (16 million kids who would otherwise go without medical care); the blind and disabled (4.9 million people who get home health care services). Clearly Congress is cutting a wide swath here.

Reprinted with special permission of North America Syndicate.

In all this squabbling over the details of Medicare and Medicaid costs, a more basic question is somehow lost: how will we, as a society, prioritize our resources? Testifying before the Senate Finance Committee in May 1995, Brookings Institution senior fellow Robert Reischauer put our options simply:

> If we allow the unrestrained growth of Medicare, we will have to accept one or a combination of three possible repercussions: the share of national resources available for other government programs will have to be reduced drastically, taxes will have to be increased significantly, and/or government deficits will have to increase, thereby eroding the economy's long-run potential.

He concluded, "None of these is acceptable."

But others are not so sure. "I would try to rebalance this, "argues Jack Meyer, a health economist at New Directions for Policy. "Medicare and Medicaid cuts total $450 billion—that's nearly half of the total cuts they're shooting for to balance the budget. That's asking a lot of health care."

If anything, Congress seems determined to avoid actually having to shape those priorities, allowing market forces to determine health care for the elderly. Though no one's quite sure how the "free market" will affect services for this vulnerable population—i.e., insurers may not be thrilled to enroll someone in my Uncle Bernard's condition—no one seems averse to experimenting on them. . . .

Making Judgments Amidst Confusion

Seniors are being asked to weigh their finances and health, and to use that information to evaluate the Republicans' plans for reduced Medicare spending. If Republicans get their way and convert Medicare into a voucher system, these seniors will also be asked to do a risk assessment, a kind of informal cost-benefit analysis, betting on their health over the next year. They will then be asked to use their voucher to buy the insurance plan that will best meet their predicted needs. It's a tall order.

Given the complexity of the issues involved, I worry about my Aunt May and her husband Bernard's ability to make that judgment; I worry about my own ability to make it. I worry because there isn't a lot of information out there about how vouchers or the Medicare cuts in general will play out in daily life. I worry that my ignorance on the topic leaves me susceptible to misleading sound bites. I worry because often I simply don't have time to try to make sense of the jargon and rhetoric. I worry that the GOP is counting on that.

But stepping into the Medicare/Medicaid discussion is like entering a labyrinth. The language of debate is insular, convoluted, and perplexing. This is true at the high end—the policy papers—as well as the low end—the Medicare user's statement, which apparently engenders such widespread confusion that every single one arrives with the banner headline: THIS IS NOT A BILL! As niece and layperson, trying to answer a simple question—how will this affect my family?—I was getting nowhere. As reporter, I made more than forty phone calls to health care administrators, advocates, and think-tank analysts, urging them to define, elaborate, reword, and explain more than two hundred pages of policy statements, before I began to at last make sense of what was at stake. It's a luxury most Americans don't have.

Just figuring out the difference between necessary services and those Medicare deems necessary requires combing through pamphlet after pamphlet and bolstering your understanding of specifics via repeated calls to the local health administration office, social workers, and geriatric-service professionals. (Setting up a Medicare 800-number was a good idea, but in practice, year-round, it's about as accessible as the IRS number on April 14.) . . .

Promises and Rhetoric

The success of the much-favored free-market voucher program hinges on seniors' confusion, on their incorrectly calculating health risks so that insurers and health maintenance organizations [HMOs] turn a profit.

Perplexed? Don't worry about it. A House Republican Conference memo suggests members eschew explanations in favor of glib promises that "Republicans are doing the right thing for America's seniors." The memo pledges to "abide by a set of core principles," but never details what these principles might be. Six times the brief bulletin spells out the preferred phraseology— "We're preserving, protecting and strengthening Medicare"—and assures wary Republicans that, "when your constituents understand this, they'll support our efforts without reservation."

That is the plan. Or rather, the strategy. And behind such rhetoric hides serious change.

In fact, Congress seems poised to accept a voucher program. Here, the government would give seniors a voucher, worth, say $4000, to go toward purchasing the private insurance of their choice. By promising seniors they get to keep the savings, economists believe this will act as an incentive to draw people into the lower-priced HMOs. What advocates of this plan don't mention is that the government will control costs by setting the value of the voucher. And its value will erode over time. According to the Democrats' Ways and Means Committee staff analysis, the government will promise seniors vouchers worth approximately $4000 in 1995, when the market value of an insurance policy is genuinely $4000. Fine. But next year, they'll give seniors a voucher worth $5000 when private insurance costs are closer to $5100, the following year the voucher will be for $5200 and private insurance policies will have risen to $5500, etc. In seven years, seniors will have paid an additional $4400. But this plan appeals to most politicians because they're almost grandfathered: constituents won't feel the pinch for a couple of years and by that time the instigators will be safely reelected. . . .

A Two-Tiered System

Some health care experts object to a voucher/HMO system because it converts a mostly egalitarian health insurance program into a two-tiered system. "If you believe that all people in this country truly have the same access to information and the power to freely make decisions—that differences in class, race, gender, access, and transportation don't exist—then you could say a free-market system would work," says Donna Yee, codirector of the National Resource Center's Institute for Health Policy at Brandeis. "But I don't buy it." Like school vouchers, such chits have the potential to exaggerate discrepancies in the quality of care rather than reduce them. Those who can afford to purchase a better health care plan by kicking in some of their own dollars will probably do so. Those who can't will have to settle for less comprehensive coverage.

And finally, there are those who argue that for-profit HMOs and vouchers, by their very nature, provide a disincentive for thorough treatment. "This shift in policy really seems to be about making it more profitable for providers," argues John Capitman [director of the National Resource Center on Diversity and Long-Term Care]. Of course, there are HMOs that are nonprofit and reputed to be quite good—like Kaiser Permanente in California and Harvard Community Health Plan—and managed care can mean local, consumer-directed, human-scale HMOs, but such beasts run counter to the fundamental free-market, competition-driven philosophy that backers, Republican and Democrat, believe will reform and save our Medicare system. . . .

More Burdens on Seniors

GOP rhetoric conflates genuine empowerment—informing patients of their options and tailoring a treatment plan to fit their needs—with the "choices" a market-driven system will make available to those who can afford them. In fact, "flexibility" and, borrowing from abortion rights activists, "choice" are the key words in the new Republican strategy of health care reform. But even in the best of circumstances, these words don't really reflect reality. "Young, healthy workers, for heaven's sakes, have great difficulty assessing their health insurance options even with the help of employers and with personnel counselors in their businesses," Congress member Jim McDermott has said. "Senior citizens will have none of these advantages as they try to select the policy that will give them the greatest protection, provided they can pay for it and can overcome the subtle strategies of the health insurance industry to direct the less healthy customers away from their companies."

Capitman of the National Resource Center also sees problems with the voucher strategy. "Elderly people—indeed most people—don't want to decide, do I go for this premium and this deduction? How do I predict how sick I might be next year?" he says, observing that many of the proposals out there shift the risk from the government to the consumer. "But these are choices seniors really don't want to make, and the possibility for them to be taken advantage of by the insurance industry increases tremendously here.". . .

Inhibiting Debate

A kind of false optimism pervades talk of the nation's health care crisis. Each proposal put forward is touted as the solution—the single, simple step that will save money and lives. We are discouraged from looking deeper. Ironically, while shrouding the debate in secrecy, the GOP peddles a plan that celebrates the "informed consumer." Patients are supposed to comprehend, and in some cases anticipate, the intricacies of their illnesses in order to make wise and cost-effective decisions about their health care. It's asking a lot. While managed care may be an effective way of reducing the cost of medical care in this country, its efficacy hinges on the development of community-based, not-for-profit group practices.

But of course, that runs counter to the very foundation of GOP reforms. Most of the proposals are based on providing economic incentives in a profit-based market system. Writing about health reform in *Tikkun* in 1994, Swarthmore psychology professor Barry Schwartz wondered what it would mean for Americans to accept such incentives. "By doing so, we accede implicitly to the view that the profit motive is the engine for producing a just distribution of health-care services, surely an odd view in light of its failure to produce a just distribution of anything else."

In the end, Congress will probably cobble together a plan that celebrates the free market and goes for conventional cost-cutting measures. Fair-market-value vouchers will be distributed (and their worth will quickly erode); seniors will be shoved into managed care; deductibles, premiums, and copayments will go up; reimbursements to doctors and hospitals will go down, slightly. These bits and pieces of the various proposals make for a circuitous route to savings, but promise to provide enough elements to complicate, and undoubtedly stymie, meaningful debate.

A few analysts are pushing for a more direct approach. Jack Meyer, [a health economist] at New Directions for Policies, would like to see the $100 Medicare deductible go up, to see wealthier seniors pay a larger premium, and to raise the eligibility level above 65 years. But some groups, like the Older Women's League, are quick to criticize any effort to make Medicare a means-tested program, observing that such a move would "erode broad-based public support for this social insurance program." And indeed, if Medicare were to transmogrify into a program for the destitute, it would soon be subject to the same slurs and slander that have characterized the attack on welfare. Newt Gingrich has already proved himself a master of divide-and-conquer techniques and must now hone that skill in a PR [public relations] push that lulls a youthful middle class into believing that the fate of the elderly may be separate from their own. GOP success hinges on their ability to convince the public that irrelevant groups are getting enormous deals from the government. But can Republicans successfully convince us that grandma is the other?

Periodical Bibliography

The following articles have been selected to supplement the diverse views presented in this chapter. Addresses are provided for periodicals not indexed in the *Readers' Guide to Periodical Literature*, the *Alternative Press Index*, or the *Social Sciences Index*.

Gary S. Becker and Isaac Ehrlich	"Social Security: Foreign Lessons," *Wall Street Journal*, March 30, 1994.
Susan Douglas	"A Bedside View of Medicare," *Progressive*, July 1995.
Howard Fineman	"MediScare," *Newsweek*, September 18, 1995.
Thomas Geoghegan	"Why Americans Don't Save," *New Republic*, July 17–24, 1995.
David Hage	"Privatizing Social Security," *U.S. News & World Report*, April 3, 1995.
William Hogeboom	"Social Security: 'Sacred Cow' of Entitlement Programs," *USA Today*, November 1995.
Michael Kinsley	"The Best Way to Fix Medicare," *Time*, September 4, 1995.
Elizabeth Kolbert	"Who Will Face the Music?" *New York Times Magazine*, August 27, 1995.
Ted Marmor	"The Medicare Solution: And Why Myths, Misinformation, and Mudslinging—from Both Parties—Won't Get Us There," *Washington Monthly*, September 1995.
Modern Maturity	Special issue on Social Security, July/August 1995.
Rob Nelson	"Fix It Now or Risk a Generational War," *Los Angeles Times*, June 12, 1995. Available from Reprints, Times Mirror Square, Los Angeles, CA 90012-3816.
Norman J. Ornstein	"Flashback," *New Republic*, July 3, 1995.
Aldona Robbins	"Salvaging Social Security," *Wall Street Journal*, July 3, 1995.
World & I	Special section on Social Security, November 1995. Available from 3600 New York Ave. NE, Washington, DC 20002.

3 CHAPTER

What Quality of Life Do Older Americans Face?

AN AGING POPULATION

Chapter Preface

For decades, retirement for many seniors meant a worry-free and leisurely life: taking up a hobby, traveling, and entertaining grandchildren. They retired with the reassurance that they could live comfortably from the combined earnings of pensions, savings, and Social Security.

However, this traditional image of retirement has lost much of its lustre, according to many observers. In the words of *U.S. News & World Report* senior editor Steven D. Kaye, "The time when pensions paid generously, when the Social Security system was strong, and when thriftiness ruled is history."

Whether or not Kaye is correct, many seniors fear that funding their retirement will prove much more difficult now than in the past. As one 59-year-old worker, who anticipated savings and Social Security to provide just one-third of her $60,000 salary, explained, "Given the finiteness of my resources, I can't think about retiring. I have no choice but to work into my seventies." According to many experts, retirees need 60 to 80 percent of their previous annual income per year to maintain their standard of living.

In order to meet retirement needs, many seniors are extending their working lives by retaining their jobs, changing careers, or finding part-time work. But experts stress that workers must plan for retirement early in their lives. According to U.S. labor secretary Robert B. Reich, workers of all ages should heed "the fundamental importance of saving for the future. We need to educate Americans about the importance of taking personal responsibility for their retirement security."

The viewpoints in the following chapter foresee what quality of life—including financial and physical well-being—awaits older Americans.

"*Retirees . . . have discovered that the secrets to happiness are as varied as their own interests.*"

Retirement Can Be Ideal

Sandra Dallas

In the following viewpoint, Sandra Dallas describes the successful retirement of several couples and individuals. Dallas maintains that people can achieve a successful retirement by preparing early and by honing personal skills and interests. Dallas is a freelance writer based in Denver, Colorado.

As you read, consider the following questions:

1. What changes did the Talleys face by retiring to a different state, according to Dallas?
2. According to Madelyn Iris, cited by the author, how can retirees succeed without a large nest egg?
3. Who are the most content of single retirees, according to Dallas?

Sandra Dallas, "Successful Retirees Tell How and Why." First printed in *New Choices: Living Even Better After 50*, February 1995. Reprinted with permission of the publisher.

Marie Sautter remembers the day she and her husband, Carl, began making plans for retirement. "He said: 'Tell me when you decide we have enough money,'" she says. "So one day I decided we did and called him at the office." Soon after that, the advertising agency where Carl worked was reorganized, and the fun disappeared from his job. In 1990 the Sautters left Houston for Breckenridge, a ski resort in the Colorado Rockies. They've never looked back.

Marie, now 59, and Carl, 73, take long morning walks in the mountains and then stop for coffee and newspapers in a café. In the afternoons, they read in front of the fire or on their veranda, which has a stunning view of the ski slopes. Both Marie and Carl are making their way through an ambitious list of classics. On a recent day, one was engrossed in Tolstoy's *War and Peace*; the other was reading Edith Wharton's *Glimpses of the Moon*.

An Army Air Forces navigator in the South Pacific during World War II, Carl makes model airplanes of that era for his grandsons, walks to classes at Colorado Mountain College and volunteers at the historic house-museum next door. Marie, a retired caterer and weaver, gardens at the museum and makes doll clothes or weaves in her home studio.

Enjoying Retirement

Seven Sautter grandchildren live two hours away and visit often. "I want them to remember happy times at Grandma's home," says Marie, pausing to help a granddaughter with her knitting. The Sautters share household jobs, such as plumbing work and kitchen cleanup. Evenings, they see friends or watch mysteries on TV and old black-and-white horror films—"awful, terrible movies," says Carl, shaking his head.

Exercise and a high-fiber, low-fat diet keep the couple healthy. (A recent purchase was a pasta machine.) And the dry air has all but eliminated Marie's asthma.

Do they enjoy retirement? "I wish I'd started when I was 10," says Carl. "We're sitting in the catbird seat." Little wonder. According to the experts, the Sautters do everything right. Good health and financial security are obvious requirements for a rewarding retirement, but that's not all it takes. Successful retirees "create a meaningful purpose and activity that transfer into some sort of identity of self. They don't isolate themselves from the outside world. If they're married, they've found ways to structure separateness," explains Sara Honn Qualls, director of the Center on Aging at the University of Colorado in Colorado Springs.

Like the Sautters, the retirees described below have discovered that the secrets to happiness are as varied as their own interests. What they all share is a readiness, even eagerness, to make things happen.

Ruth Talley, a former housekeeper, was uneasy about retiring 1,000 miles across the country when her husband, Eual, left his job as a storekeeper with Western Union in Denver. For six years the Talleys had vacationed in Watson, Arkansas, and they found its low prices, low crime and wonderful fishing a welcome change from city life. Still, living there full-time would be different. It would mean leaving behind their support system of family and friends for a new home where Ruth and her husband knew few people.

Retirement and Freedom

The exhilaration of freedom is a daily experience and the most wondrous thing about retirement. There are no tight schedules, unless one makes one's own; no getting up to an alarm clock's raucous and insistent buzz; no worry about what to wear, as casual clothes rule the day; and no agonizing over daily humdrum decisions. As one retiree put it, "The biggest decision I make now is whether to have bacon and eggs or a bowl of cereal for breakfast." With the shucking of most responsibilities, one has a chance to be a kid again. We have so many picnics, both by ourselves and with new-found friends, that my wife swears she will use as my epitaph "Life was a picnic," and it will be an accurate description.

Gerald F. Kreyche, *USA Today*, May 1993.

Ruth knew that meeting other people could be a problem—she didn't have a driver's license, which in rural Arkansas meant she was completely dependent on Eual to get anywhere. She also wondered whether it was wise to retire so young. She was 55 years old, Eual was 60, and money was tight.

Despite these misgivings, the Talleys made the leap and landed happily. They love hunting and fishing together, and Ruth, a gregarious woman, quickly made friends after she began attending a church in Watson. She also learned how to drive. A granddaughter, Karen, moved to Watson with her 2-year-old son, Brent. He was terminally ill, and Ruth devoted herself to him, enriching his life while giving herself a sense of purpose in retirement. By the time Brent died two years ago, Ruth's son and his wife were also living in the town. Together, the family shared their grief. These days, Ruth helps care for Karen's two more recent children and tends Brent's grave. Thanks to Ruth's economizing, the Talleys get by financially. "Girl," she says proudly, "I just put up 14 pints of pear preserves, 21 quarts of pears and 50 quarts of pickles."

As the Talleys have found, although a sizable nest egg can be helpful, it's not essential. "A lot of people did not have money before they retired," points out Madelyn Iris, associate director of education at the Buehler Center on Aging at Northwestern University in Evanston, Illinois. "They make do. They live within their means. They have the time to shop outlet stores and use coupons." Besides, she adds: "They're not anticipating trips to Paris. They want to go to St. Louis."

Getting Good Advice

A growing number of retirees are taking advantage of new corporate programs. After attending a Prudential Insurance Company of America seminar for employees with his wife, Rosanna, Leo White was persuaded that although the value of stock investments may fluctuate, the principal is less likely to be eroded by inflation than assets kept in bonds or the bank. The seminar series also encouraged White, an information-systems manager, to stay busy once he stopped work. "Knock off time for meals and sleep, and there still are a lot of hours to fill," says White.

When he retired last summer at age 58, White joined two retirement groups near his home in Boonton Township, New Jersey. The Happy Walkers exercise regularly. The Golden Boys, a mutual support group for men, plans outings such as an evening at a dinner theater or a field trip to a zinc mine.

Early Planning

Ideally, "good, sound retirement planning should begin when you enter the work force," says Monica Brown, assistant manager for the Work Force Education program at the American Association of Retired Persons. Of course, few people are that provident. Mel Carter was. An art teacher and coordinator of fine arts at the Community College of Denver, Carter had a retirement plan in place by the time he was 30. Each month, he put aside $150 until he had enough for a down payment on a house, which he fixed up and rented. Gradually he acquired other rental properties.

He also developed his art skills, always intending to devote full time to painting after he retired. When Carter was 48 years old, the college offered him early retirement; he seized the opportunity and was able to stop working with little change in income or activity. "Because I worried then," says Carter, "I don't worry now."

Five years after retiring, Carter is well known in Denver as a figure painter and landscape artist. Some work he sells through galleries—the American ambassador to Austria is among the purchasers. Other paintings he donates to charity; one was recently auctioned off to raise money for AIDS research. When Carter isn't painting or teaching art, he travels all over the world, making sketches that he compiles into personal art books or uses for future paintings. On weekends at home, he haunts garage sales in search of more architectural relics for his 22-room house. Because he is single and has little family, Carter says, "having a network of friends is important." He regularly calls out-of-town friends and sends them papers he writes about his trips, illustrated with his watercolors.

Retirees generally are realistic about their expectations, knowing, for instance, that "you can't travel and see your grandkids all the time. You have to transfer the meaning of work to some other activity in your life, paid or unpaid," says Qualls at the Center on Aging.

Charles Daly really plunged in after retiring from government service. Intending to spend his time bodysurfing and golfing, he moved to Cape Carteret, North Carolina, on the Atlantic Ocean. Soon he was looking for something to do with his spare time and ended up serving three terms as mayor.

When the town of 1,500 was threatened by a hurricane, Daly organized the evacuation. In the process, he discovered that many of the town's older residents who lived alone needed help. Once again he got busy, forming a widowed persons group. The members meet monthly to socialize and help one another with the problems of single life. Daly, a 76-year-old whose wife died four years ago, is a member himself. "Whether it's politics or carving duck decoys, you've got to have something to get you out of bed in the morning, especially if you've lost a mate," he says.

Living Alone Actively

Among single retirees, the most content are usually the ones who make an extra effort to be independent. When Marjorie Carter retired last year as manager of a Lake Forest, Illinois, real-estate office, she moved to Santa Fe to be near her son, Neil. "But I didn't come here expecting to be taken care of," notes Carter, now 66. She brought along "a list of ways I intended to make my niche here." Most of the list will have to wait. Carter is too busy reading for a book club she joined, playing her new grand piano, and building a patio beside her house with the help of friends. Neil is lucky if Carter can work him in every two weeks.

"I am thoroughly happy," she says, echoing the words of other successful retirees. In fact, she may have hit on the basic secret of all of them: "I don't think of it as retirement, I think of it as a lifestyle change."

"Retiring is probably the greatest myth that has been perpetuated on the American public and probably does the most harm."

Retirement May Not Be Ideal

Florence Tauber and Al Tauber

According to Florence Tauber and Al Tauber, the accepted age of retirement has nothing to do with a person's ability to work, and policies should be changed to encourage working beyond age sixty-five. The Taubers maintain that because of financial constraints, such as lower purchasing power, inflation, and higher health costs, retirement is not a practical goal. The authors assert that the retirement years should be a period of continued work rather than one of inactivity. Florence Tauber and Al Tauber are, respectively, president of and researcher for Third Age Press in Portland, Oregon.

As you read, consider the following questions:

1. How many retirees reenter the job market, according to the authors, and why do they return to work?
2. According to Alex Comfort, cited by the authors, what two types of people are "really happy conventionally retired"?
3. In the authors' opinion, who are the "retirement winners"?

Excerpted from Florence and Al Tauber, *Over the Hill at 40 and Other Outrageous Lies* (Portland, OR: Third Age Press, 1993). Reprinted by permission.

Retiring is probably the greatest myth that has been perpetuated on the American public and probably does the most harm. One has to recognize that retirement is a political device imposed by one group on another for the purposes of control.

Retiring was invented by Prince Otto von Bismarck in 1883, when he established the world's first state system of social security in order to weaken the appeal of socialism. He set retirement age at 70 and did not expect that the average worker would ever receive a pension, since life expectancy in Germany at that time was about 45. German officials later reduced the retirement age to 65.

The selection of age 65 for use as a demarcation between middle and old age was an arbitrary one. It had nothing to do with a person's ability to work. This numerical definition of old age has been adhered to for social purposes and as a means for determining the point of eligibility for various services for older people. Employment should be a matter of choice after 65.

One-third of retirees reenter the job market within two years of retirement. Blue collar workers go back most likely for financial reasons, while white collar employees are more likely to reenter because they enjoy their work.

Earnings Limits

The ability to work is hampered by the earnings limits for recipients of social security. The earnings limit was established as a matter of public policy to drive older people out of the labor force to make way for younger workers. That need no longer exists and it is detrimental to the person who needs to work to live.

The policy was very effective. In 1948 one-half of all American men 65 plus worked; in 1989 only 16 percent.

The Third Age [retirement] population should aggressively pressure Congress and the President to remove earnings restrictions and recognize the multiple benefits that a Third Age labor force brings to the market place. Among them are contributions to taxes and reduction in health care costs resulting from a more vital older population.

In 1935 when our social security system was established 65-year-olds lived 12.5 years longer. Our politicians made a generous social security offer to workers just like Bismarck, predicated on the fact that very few would live to take advantage of it. Now 72-year-olds will live 12.5 years longer. As a result, our government now faces the inability to keep its promises and we can expect only a continual reduction of benefits over time. This is another battle that the Third Age population has to prepare to fight vigorously. . . .

Science and medicine long has recognized that age has only limited relevance to the general function, health, mental capacity, physical endurance and creativity of people. Throughout life, age is only a convenient and inaccurate indication of a person's physical and mental status.

When our country was an agricultural society few retired. But as we have become more industrialized the idea of rewarding labor with leisure benefits after a fixed employment period became public policy. And it was effective. Look at the figures: In 1900, 70 percent of men over 65 were employed. Sixty years later in 1960 only 35 percent were employed after 65. By 1975 only 22 percent were working and in 1983 only 17 percent.

Retirement: Dramatic Change Ahead

As baby boomers and others hear about proposed cuts in Social Security and Medicare and anticipate modest or uncertain pensions, their realistic, if somewhat gloomy, assessment increasingly is: "I won't be able to afford to retire."

Retirement as Americans have come to know it—a time to turn off the alarm clock, collect Social Security, and enjoy years of leisure, perhaps in the Sun Belt—appears poised for dramatic shifts. The need for extra money and the desire to be productive and useful cannot be programmed to end at age 65.

Somehow the work force must be restructured to accommodate these new realities. Instead of the usual all-or-nothing approach—full-time jobs requiring 40 or 50 hours a week—managers could create more part-time positions. Although reduced schedules are usually viewed as a way to meet the needs of parents with young children, they would equally serve middle-aged workers caring for older relatives, and those over 65 who are eager to work, though not a full week.

Marilyn Gardner, *Christian Science Monitor*, December 14, 1995.

Indicative of the negative impact of retiring is the high suicide rate for aged men. The figures show that the suicide rate of men 55 to 64 is 22.5 per one hundred thousand from 65 to 74—28.4, from 75 to 84—41.4, 85 and over—50.2. A total of 37,000 men over the age 65 killed themselves in the period 1980 to 1986.

Both white and blue collar workers suffer from loss of self-esteem if they don't have a consuming activity to absorb them after retirement. The solution is to retire into work and start another career or volunteer for worthwhile activities.

Alex Comfort, author of *A Good Age*, reports that only two kinds of folk are really happy conventionally retired: Those who were always lazy, and those who have waited a lifetime to devote themselves to a consuming, non-fantasy interest for which they have studied, prepared and planned, lacking only the time to do it the way they wanted.

Beginning in the late 1980s the trend of retiring at 65 reversed. According to records of the U.S. Bureau of Labor Statistics, in 1988 among men age 60, 68.8 percent were still in the work force. The next year the percentage had jumped to 70.7 and has stayed there. Profound changes in American society have caused the reversal. Among them is the factor that married couples are putting off starting a family, leaving them with children to raise when they reach early retirement age.

There are other economic forces at work. Generous early retirement incentives, popular in the 1980's as a payroll-cutting device, are reported to be declining. Even more crucial is the fact that employers are shifting more and more of the cost of retiree health insurance to employees, giving middle-aged workers a strong incentive to stay on the job.

The Economics of Aging

The fact of the matter is that retirement is not a practical goal for the majority of people given the economics of living longer. As you get older you will find your income curving downward if it is not augmented by additional income. Two out of five older persons, some twelve million people, live in poverty or close to its edge. The proportion of retirees receiving private pension income increased to 16.9 percent in 1990. Only a tiny fraction of these pensions are indexed to protect against inflation. These are the persons considered to be retirement winners. The wealthiest 20 percent prospered the most, getting nearly half of all elderly income; the poorest one-fifth got less than 4 percent.

Two million women who live alone are below the poverty line. While 3.7 million older persons are officially declared poor, another 8.1 million are considered near poor. Any sudden economic reversal could push them into poverty. Altogether, 40 percent of the thirty million people 65 and older have incomes that are no more than double the poverty line. Even retirement winners can expect to lose some ground eventually from ebbing earning power, loss of pension benefits when a spouse dies, chronic illness and dwindling purchasing power due to inflation.

In 1991, the maximum Social Security benefit for someone retiring at age 65 was $1,022 a month or $12,264 a year—hardly enough to support even a modest lifestyle. And at a 5 percent rate of inflation it will take $2,650 in twenty years to equal the purchasing power of $1,000 today. When you consider the combined effect of interest and taxes, Treasury bills and other interest-bearing investments probably won't provide the growth you need.

With increasing health costs over the past decade (more than doubled) and elevated drug prices (the cost of drugs increased

152 percent), additional unplanned financial demands will be made on diminishing incomes and purchasing power. More than 85 percent of all people 65 and over take at least one prescription drug regularly.

Financial myths say that you will not need as much money during retirement as you do now. Not true! You will have more expenses for travel, leisure activities, hobbies etc. You can also plan on increasing medical expenses. Generally the average income from Social Security will not be adequate to the needs of the recipient. Medicare pays less than half of a retiree's medical bills. Many employers are cutting back on medical coverage for retirees because of costs.

In the face of these negative facts, what can aging people do to live better? Part of the answer is to make your voice heard by lawmakers to terminate punitive restrictions on income by persons who work while receiving Social Security benefits. Many people will elect to work until 70 and beyond. Older, experienced people are finding employment for their specialized skills.

Instead of thinking about retirement as a period of inactivity, think instead of it as an opportunity to discover new career ideas.

"Three-quarters of Americans over age 20 will have less than half of what they will need when they retire."

The Outlook for Future Retirees Is Bleak

Leslie Eaton

Many Americans are anxious that their retirement years will be hampered by financial hardship. In the following viewpoint, Leslie Eaton asserts that almost all future retirees will not achieve the percentage of annual working income needed to retire comfortably. Eaton contends that as the large baby boomer population nears retirement age, the problem of an inadequate retirement nest egg could become a crisis in America. Eaton is the mutual funds editor for *Barron's*, a weekly financial newspaper.

As you read, consider the following questions:

1. According to Eaton, how many households lack pension coverage?
2. What has happened to traditional pension plans, according to the author?
3. In Eaton's opinion, why are many workers uninformed about retirement investing?

Excerpted from Leslie Eaton, "Cloudy Sunset: A Grim Surprise Awaits Future Retirees," *Barron's*, July 12, 1993. Reprinted by permission of *Barron's*, ©1993 Dow Jones & Company, Inc. All rights reserved worldwide.

The good news is: You can probably accumulate enough to retire on—given a lot of luck, time and investment smarts.

The bad news is: Those attributes are not widely distributed among the American populace, huge chunks of which will not have enough to make ends meet once they retire.

The *really* bad news is: All you folks who did the right things may well end up paying for the out-of-luck, the out-of-time, and the investment innocents. And it could cost you very big bucks.

If all of the above is news to you, then like most Americans you haven't focused on the seismic shifts that have been taking place in our society since 1983: shifts in demographics, in business practices, in government regulations and in pension programs. Combined, they make your retirement outlook mighty different from your parents'—and bode even worse for your kids'. Indeed, as the studies and forecasts pile up, some doom-and-gloomers are predicting a retirement crisis that will dwarf the burning issues of our day. Except, as [former] SEC [Securities and Exchange Commission] Commissioner Carter Beese points out, this crisis "will have a much greater effect on individuals' quality of life than the deficit or health-care reform ever will."

Why People Should Worry

Some bulletins from the retirement front: A government-sponsored survey released in June 1993 found that 40% of people aged 51–61 expect to have no retirement income except Social Security. About 20% now have no real assets. And many of those surveyed, who have a median income of $37,500, are helping to support their parents, their kids, even their grand-children.

Younger and wealthier Americans may not be in much better shape—and there are a lot more of them. Results of a major study—published [in *Barron's*] for the first time—by consultants WEFA Group and Arthur D. Little (and, let it be said, paid for by fund company Oppenheimer Management), concludes that three-quarters of Americans over age 20 will have less than half of what they will need when they retire. It could be a lot less, if financial markets falter, Social Security falls apart, or, worst of all, retirees failed to get a pension when they were working. And right now, according to WEFA, almost half of all American households have absolutely no pension coverage.

The study's projections, derived by feeding federal government data into WEFA's econometric model, aren't great for even some of the most well-to-do. They're far worse for some groups, particularly single women of all ages and incomes, some of whom will have only 40% of the money they'll need to maintain their current standards of living.

But the really ugly numbers, from a political point of view, come when you examine the great bulge of middle-income baby boomers. Households headed by 30–34-year-olds now number about 13.2 million—more than twice the number of those 55–59, or 60–64. A peek at the biggest slab of these boomers—married and making from $25,000 to $50,000 a year—finds that if current trends continue, they're likely to have less than 60% of the income they'll need when they stop working.

Ax their pensions and their comfort level falls to 20%. They won't be happy. They will vote. And politicians are highly unlikely to let them all starve—or riot—in the streets of Miami Beach.

"A lot of people grew up watching their parents retire with Social Security and a pension providing a significant portion of what they needed to live," says Bob Doll, Oppenheimer's director of equity investments. "Those people think, 'Mom and Dad made it, therefore I'm going to make it.' But unless somebody's coming with a pot of gold from the sky, they won't."

To be sure, all the polls, studies and surveys pointing to a crisis could be overstating the problem; though carried out by independent organizations, most such efforts have been funded by financial-services companies that have a vested interest in scaring people into buying more of their wares. On the other hand, the basic trends fueling retirement problems are plenty scary on their own, and cause concern among academics, actuaries, financial planners and other professional worrywarts.

It's also true that the full effects of these trends won't be felt for several years, and that the vast bulk of baby boomers won't retire for 30 years. A lot could happen between now and then. American corporations *could* return to providing generous, traditional, expensive pension coverage. American politicians *could* try to mandate better benefits before there's a crisis, or expand government retirement programs—despite the behemoth budget deficit. American retirees *could* suddenly decide to embrace austerity and take pride in subsistence-level living.

But let's get real. One more plausible solution is that Americans take responsibility for their own retirements and become better investors. The trend so far isn't terribly encouraging, but modest evidence indicates that education efforts can have some effect. This solution also presupposes the financial markets' cooperation.

At the Age of Retirement

There's an even simpler solution: People just won't be able to retire. "You're already seeing some manifestations of this—the person behind the counter at McDonald's or at the grocery checkout is not necessarily a teenager any more," says Eric Russell, director of defined-contribution services at consultants Frank Russell Co. "There's a whole new workforce that doesn't have the income it needs to retire."

But the trend has been toward ever-earlier retirement. The U.S. Bureau of Labor Statistics reports that the percentage of men over 66 still in the work force has been declining since 1970. Back then, about 29% of such men worked; by '91, only 17% did. In fact, though people will have to work longer to be eligible for full Social Security benefits—the age test climbs to 67 by 2022—many people now take their benefits at age 62.

And not always by choice. Forced early retirement has been a favorite tool for cost-cutting at American corporations from GM and IBM on down. That may change; some seers predict a short-age of skilled workers when the small "baby buster" group hits middle age. But a "work 'til you drop" future is a far cry from the leisured retirement most Americans have come to expect. . . .

The Baby Boomer Factor

[Baby] boomers now make up 30% of the population, dwarf-ing the generations before and behind them. And they're likely to live a long, long time. Babies born after World War II have a life expectancy of 63 for men and 68 for women. Those who reach retirement age can expect to stick around a lot longer. In the mid-'Fifties, retiring men enjoyed an average 13 more years of life, women 16 years. Today, retiring men can expect to live about 15 years, women close to 20. . . .

Combine the boomer bulge and longer life expectancy and you get the graying of America. Arthur D. Little reckons that while the number of people under age 20 will stay relatively constant until 2030, the number of people over 65 will soar to 21% of the population, from 13% today.

Bad News for Social Security

You need not be a professional prognosticator to predict that this will not have happy consequences for programs such as So-cial Security and Medicare. For while a lot more people will be eligible to draw on them, far fewer young people will be around to pour money in. In 1990, according to the Social Security Ad-ministration, more than three workers were contributing to the program for each person receiving benefits. In 30 years, there will be just two workers per beneficiary.

Why does that matter? Because, despite what politicians and current beneficiaries tell you, Social Security is not a savings or investment program; it is an income-transfer scheme. Nobody who's now receiving benefits put in enough to cover what they're taking out, even if their contributions had been invested at a reasonable return. Current workers pay for the benefits to the old and disabled.

Fortunately, at the moment more money is flowing in at the

top of the tank than is draining out the bottom, thanks to the 1983 reforms that "rescued" the program. Unfortunately, the "surplus" isn't being invested on behalf of future beneficiaries; instead, it is offsetting the federal deficit. Even more unfortunately, the aging of America will likely mean that the fund will drain ever faster, while the money coming in could slow to a trickle. By the Social Security trustees' own estimates, the trust fund could have negative cash flow by 1997 and could be out of money by 2017 in its worst-case scenario, which some commentators think isn't gloomy enough. . . .

Boomers' Threatened Standard of Living

Unless the nation magically undergoes a sudden, vaulting—and sustained—surge in productivity, your children and grandchildren will be faced with a Hobbesian choice: Either they support vastly higher taxes on their own incomes or sharply cut back Social Security and Medicare to their parents and grandparents.

Don't delude yourself by thinking that private pension plans and IRAs [individual retirement accounts] are going to bail you out— at least not at the rate that boomers are pumping money into them. Says B. Douglas Bernheim, an authority on savings trends, "The typical baby-boom household is saving at one-third the rate required to finance a standard of living during retirement comparable to a standard of living that it enjoys before retirement."

Christopher Byron, *Esquire*, July 1995.

More than 40% of retired Americans depend on Social Security for less than half of their income. Most of these retired Americans are living off their private pensions. The total sum of private-sector benefits paid to retirees has soared to $138 billion in 1989 from $19 billion in 1975, according to the Employee Benefit Research Institute [EBRI].

On average, the government figures, private pensions replace 15%–20% of retirees' final salaries, vs. anywhere from 10% to 70% for Social Security (the lower the wage, the more Social Security replaces). While few retirees would allow that their pensions are lavish—and they're not usually indexed for inflation—most would probably agree that these pensions have made the difference between ease and want.

Traditional Pension Plans and 401(k)s

But future retirees aren't likely to have it so good. Traditional pension plans have stopped growing, victims of corporate cutbacks and increased government regulation, as well as a more mobile workforce that changes jobs frequently and doesn't stick around at any company long enough to build up a big pension. The number of people working at companies that offer traditional pension plans—mostly the industrial giants—has been flat since the early 'Eighties; the number of people who are really covered has actually declined a bit, the Employee Benefit Research Institute reports. Between 1985 and 1989, the number of traditional pension plans plunged almost 22%, with the major drops—affecting three million people—occurring at companies that employ fewer than 1,000 people, says EBRI's Celia Silverman.

What smaller and service-sector companies do tend to offer, and in increasing numbers, are defined-contribution retirement plans. These come in a wide variety of flavors, from 401(k)s to profit-sharing plans. Companies may give employees a certain percentage of their salaries to be invested for retirement; they may encourage employees to save for themselves by matching their retirement nest eggs; or they may just let workers accumulate assets in a tax-deferred savings plan. Whether generous or stingy, these plans let workers know what they have right now—but make no promises about how much people will have when they retire.

The number of these plans soared in the 'Eighties, zooming from about 200 in 1975 to 600 or so in 1989, according to EBRI. Meanwhile, the number of people for whom this is their main pension plan more than tripled, to 14 million from four million, which means that by 1989, more than a third of workers who had pension plans were in defined-contribution programs.

The change is even more striking if you look at where the money is—and where it's been going. While assets in traditional pension plans climbed to almost $1 trillion, thanks to the 'Eighties bull market, defined-contribution assets have zoomed even faster, and by '89 hit $688 billion. But while traditional plans had 60% of the assets, they got only a quarter of the contributions—far more money flowed into defined-contribution plans.

And those trends have continued, according to Greenwich Associates, which surveys large pension plans every year. Defined-contribution programs account for an increasing amount of pension-plan assets, and while traditional plans suffered a negative net cash flow, 401(k) plans were raking it in.

The Risk to Companies

For companies, the allure of defined-contribution plans is plain. When employers promise workers specific benefits, they have to put aside money to cover them. If the market tanks or their investment manager turns out to be a dud, companies have to cough up more dough. There are lots of regulations, plus hefty fees to the troubled federal pension-insurance agency.

By comparison, defined-contribution plans are a cheap treat. All a company has to do is set up a savings program with a number of investment options, make sure enough lower-paid employees participate to keep the thing tax exempt, and maybe contribute some money to the kitty. Whether workers make good investment decisions or bad ones, whether the securities markets soar or crash, the company isn't on the hook. In fact, in many plans, companies don't have to pay up for employees who don't have the sense—or the disposable income—to save for themselves.

All of which might be okay—if employees knew that they were responsible for their retirement futures, and knew what to do about it. But by all accounts, most don't have a clue. As Cindy Hounsell, a lawyer with the nonprofit Pension Rights Center, notes, even people who happily watch the money build up in their 401(k) plans somehow don't quite realize that they substitute for benefits that companies used to guarantee. And since for most people, the money in their defined-contribution plans is more moolah than they've ever seen in their lives, they don't realize that it's far less than employers would have to pony up for traditional pensions—and far less than they will need to live on.

Almost a third of the people who could participate in a 401(k) or other retirement-savings plan don't, according to EBRI data. And even those who do participate don't always intend to use the money solely for retirement. A Gallup poll done for insurer John Hancock found that more than a quarter of those who do kick in plan to use the money for education or buying a house. About 14% of those allowed to borrow against their retirement plans had already done so—mostly to buy cars—and another 14% expected to in the next two years. If they couldn't use the money for nonretirement purposes, more than 25% of the participants told pollsters, they wouldn't contribute at all.

When people get access to that big wad of pension money—because they retire or change jobs—more than a third spend it all, EBRI reports. Only 11% put it into another retirement plan. The rest do a little of both. . . .

Investment Know-How

But before you go blaming the victims, who after all are bearing all the risk, keep in mind that few workers realize that they ought to know about investing. Certainly neither the government nor their employers have told them so. "When we moved into the defined-contribution environment," Eric Russell explains, "the laws were such that companies were afraid to communicate" with employees for fear that they would become legally liable. "Fundamentally, nobody ever told participants that this was now their responsibility," he continues. "No wonder they're not paying attention."

Even now, plan participants get little information—and what they do get is often unintelligible. Historically, companies have spent almost nothing on employee education, and even today, consultants at Dalbar in Boston found that communication remains a miniscule cost. . . .

The 70% Goal

As the Oppenheimer study shows, participating in a pension plan and investing the money more aggressively are just about the only things individuals can do to help build up the pile of assets they'll need to retire on.

The study assumes that at retirement, everyone will need about 70% of the income they averaged during their last five working years. That figure, common in the financial-planning business, basically backs out the costs of going to a job every day, explains Oppenheimer's Bob Doll.

Seventy percent sounds high at first blush, especially to those who think of their own elderly parents or grandparents, mortgages paid off, living quietly for their bridge games and a weekly trip to church. But remember that people are getting a later start on things like having their families and buying homes, so they may still have big debts when they retire. Also, leisure activities can be expensive, especially if you plan to travel or move to a condominium with monthly fees. Taxes aren't likely to go down; health-care costs are likely to go up, whatever Hillary Clinton says. And everyone's going to live a good long time.

How will people come up with the income they'll need? First off, of course, there's Social Security. But even without cutbacks, the benefits are slated to reach a maximum of about $17,000 in 2010 (in '92 dollars), which will leave a lot of people short. Then there are personal savings—which are low, and tend to be in cash, rather than in investments that beat inflation.

At best, the people at WEFA figure, Social Security and savings will provide not quite half of what retirees will need—and only if they're married, already have low incomes and are over 55. For most of us, those two legs of the proverbial retirement stool will provide far less, with the hardest-hit group relatively well-to-do women between the ages of 30 and 44 (they'll get around 15%).

So the most important thing you can do is have a pension. Any pension. For those now over 50, a traditional pension is most useful. But for those who have more time to see their investments grow, a defined-contribution plan will provide the bulk of their retirement income. Assuming that many people will have a little of both—a small traditional pension plus a 401(k), the

WEFA model finds that many households will get 50%–60% of what they need to retire. Young men with lots of income and a long time horizon get close to 100%; women who now make $25,000–$50,000, in almost every age group, get the short end of the stick (40%–45%).

How do you reach 100% of your "comfort level"? Lots of advice-mongers will tell you to scrimp, save and double your savings rate to 10% of pre-tax income. But as the WEFA model shows, that alone won't make much difference. For example, a pair of 33-year-olds now making $75,000 between them is likely to end up with 70% of what they need to retire (if they have pensions). If they double their savings, they'll get 74%. Great. The improvement for older people and poorer people is even less thrilling. . . .

Anger About Retirement Money

In all likelihood, current trends will continue. Americans will keep getting older, retiring earlier and living longer, while their traditional pensions dwindle and their conservatively invested 401(k)s don't generate the returns they need. And they'll be angry. "As people realize they can't afford to retire, you'll hear outcries from organized groups," predicts Eric Russell. "They'll be screaming that their pensions are not delivering on their promises."

Meanwhile, there will be fewer active workers to contribute to government kitties. And so taxes on the well-to-do retired are likely to keep going up.

"It's going to affect everyone, top to bottom," declares Bob Doll. "Even if you're the only one on the planet who's solved the problem, you've got to assume that Uncle Sam has your telephone number and your Social Security number. They can get you."

"Most baby boomers are likely to enjoy higher real incomes in retirement than their parents."

The Outlook for Future Retirees May Be Bright

Joyce Manchester

Baby boomers are likely to enjoy higher incomes during retirement than members of the previous generation, Joyce Manchester argues in the following viewpoint. Manchester cites a September 1993 Congressional Budget Office study to support her assertion that baby boomers could, at the least, be as prosperous in retirement as their parents are now. Manchester contends that factors such as increasing wages, more women in the workforce, and inheritance of assets stand to give baby boomers adequate retirement incomes. Manchester, a former assistant economics professor at Dartmouth College, is a principal analyst for the Congressional Budget Office in Washington, D.C.

As you read, consider the following questions:

1. At what age did current retirees acquire most of their pension benefits and private assets, according to Manchester?
2. In Manchester's opinion, what will be the effects of baby boomers' real wage growth?
3. What was the savings behavior of baby boomers' parents, according to the author?

Excerpted from Joyce Manchester, "Baby Boomers in Retirement: An Early Perspective," *Retirement in the Twenty-first Century: Ready or Not?* (Washington, DC: Employee Benefit Research Institute, 1994). Reprinted with permission of EBRI.

Many people are concerned that, in retirement, the baby boom generation will place unduly large demands on private and public resources. One reason is the sheer number of Americans born between 1946 and 1964. This bulge is expected to raise the share of the population that is aged 65 and over from about 12 percent in 1990 to about 20 percent in 2030, when the youngest baby boomer is 66 years old. Pressures will be felt in funding Social Security and private pensions and in providing health care to older people. A second reason for the concern is the lower saving rates of recent years, which reduce the odds that sufficient resources will be available to provide for the baby boomers' retirement.

The Congressional Budget Office (CBO) released a study in September 1993 that finds baby boomers, on average, could have at least as much real income and wealth in retirement as their parents' generation now has. Their saving to date is similar to that of their parents as young adults. As a whole, baby boomers have higher real incomes and more wealth than their parents had as young adults, although some demographic groups have not fared as well as others. For the most part, the parents of baby boomers, now close to or just past retirement age, seem to have adequate financial resources in retirement, reflecting in part transfer programs available to essentially all of them and unanticipated gains on housing assets rather than systematic financial planning. As long as real wages continue to grow, Social Security and private pensions remain intact, and health care expenditures do not swamp other gains, most baby boomers are likely to enjoy higher real incomes in retirement than their parents.

Too Soon to Predict

Of course, it is far too soon to predict the financial situation of baby boomers in retirement. Even though the older boomers have completed almost one-half of their working years, they are just entering the period of life when most of the financial preparations for retirement take place. It would not be surprising to find different wealth profiles of baby boomers 10 years to 20 years from now as they get much closer to their retirement years and have more information on which to base their saving decisions. Indeed, most of the pension benefits and private assets of the current retirees were acquired after they were older than the boomers are now. Moreover, baby boomers could inherit substantial amounts of wealth from their parents over the next 20 years to 30 years.

Recognize, however, that CBO is asking a restricted question in this study—whether the baby boomers' income and wealth in retirement will exceed that of their parents. The answer to that restricted question appears to be yes, but that does not imply that baby boomers are saving enough. If boomers simply reach the income of their parents' generation, the economy will show no progress and the standard of living will stagnate. The way to increase growth is for baby boomers, their parents, and the generation following the boomers to save more, through lower government deficits and higher rates of saving.

Other studies of future retirement incomes have used higher standards, although they are not related to any specific concern about overall national saving. Some suggest that baby boomers might try to maintain some proportion of their preretirement standards of living when they retire, with the proportion ranging up to 100 percent. Full replacement of preretirement incomes is probably a higher standard than current retirees have met, and we have no way of knowing what replacement ratio boomers would find acceptable. The CBO study does not examine how boomers' retirement income might relate to their preretirement income.

Boomers Will Thrive

The baby boomers will retire to a life of comfort and prosperity far beyond that of today's seniors. Their average preretirement income will rise significantly, thanks to the continued "middle-classing" of America and to the benefits of bimodalism. That real income will stretch further than it would today, because of automation and economies of scale, which will soon reduce the cost of goods as measured by the working time required to earn them. Thus, on average, the baby boomers will leave their working years with a much larger retirement fund and far more real assets than are available even to today's affluent seniors. Their health will be better, most likely far better, than we can now predict by straight-line extrapolation from today's medical practices, and the rise of smorgasbord benefits all but guarantees that boomers in two-income families will enjoy an unprecedentedly comfortable and secure old age.

Marvin Cetron, *Omni*, January 1991.

These concerns notwithstanding, CBO's findings stand in contrast to the claims of some that the baby boomers will certainly face hard times in retirement. Such assertions focus on the slowing of real wage growth, the future financial deterioration of the Social Security system, the decline in defined benefit pension plans, low private saving rates, and possible declines in the value of housing. CBO acknowledges those trends but also recognizes that real wages are still growing, the work force is more highly educated, and the participation rate of women in the labor force has increased. All of these factors portend increases in household incomes of baby boomers in retirement, in part by making greater accumulation of assets possible during their working years.

Comparing Baby Boomers with Their Parents

CBO's findings show that baby boomers in general are financially better off than their parents' generation was as young adults. Both real household income and the ratio of household wealth to income are higher, on average, for baby boomers aged 25-44 in 1989 than was true of young adults aged 25-44 in 1959 and 1962.

The advantage of older boomers is even greater than that of younger boomers. For the group aged 25-34, median household income in 1989 dollars is 35 percent higher than it was for a similar group in 1959—$30,000 in 1989 and $22,300 in 1959. The slightly older group, aged 35-44, reports substantially larger gains, with median inflation-adjusted household income 53 percent above that of the corresponding group in 1959, rising from $25,100 to $38,400. Median household wealth in real terms is about 50 percent higher in 1989 than it was in 1962 for the younger group and about 85 percent higher for the older group.

Even more striking is the finding that the median ratio of wealth to income is higher now than it was for young adults in 1962. Among households in the 25-34 age bracket in which the head of household is not married, the median ratio of wealth to income has more than tripled. Among married couples in that age bracket, the median ratio has more than doubled. The rise in the median ratio is less pronounced for those in the 35-44 age bracket, but an increase is still evident. The median ratio rises 11 percent for unmarried heads of households and 16 percent for married couples.

These gains in household income and wealth have come despite changes in household composition that in some cases work against the betterment of household finances. For example, a much larger share of households is now headed by unmarried people who may be divorced, widowed, or never married. In 1959, an unmarried person headed just 14 percent of households in the 25-34 age group. By 1989, that proportion had more than tripled to 46 percent.

More Educated Baby Boomers

At the same time, the increased number of women in the labor force and higher educational attainment among baby boomers help to increase household incomes and wealth. The proportion of married couples with two earners has risen from 39 percent to 69 percent among households headed by a married person aged 35–44. Also, many more baby boomers are completing high school or college. The proportion of households headed by a person aged 35–44 with a high school degree has risen from 40 percent to 58 percent. For the same age group, the share of households headed by a person with four years of college has risen from 11 percent to 30 percent.

Exceptions to the general improvement in the financial situation of young adults point to those groups that have not shared in the economic prosperity of the past 30 years. Those households with heads aged 25–34 without a high school degree report lower median household income in 1989 than in 1959 after adjusting for inflation, although today's dropouts probably have fewer skills than did those of the early 1960s. Households headed by unmarried individuals aged 25–34 with children report median income about one-third the size of married couples with children and about one-twentieth as much wealth. Married couples aged 25–34 with only one earner report about two-thirds as much wealth in 1989 as in 1962. Wealth among non-homeowners aged 25–34 has not changed much since 1962 and has actually declined among nonhomeowners aged 35–44.

CBO has analyzed only changes in financial well-being as measured by income and wealth. Thus, our study does not address many "quality of life" issues that surely are of great importance when comparing how baby boomers live today with how their parents lived three decades ago or with how the boomers will live 30 years or 40 years into the future.

The large increase in women's participation in the labor force in recent decades may mean more family income and many more opportunities for women today and in the future. At the same time, this development also imposes strains on families who must set up child care arrangements outside the home and juggle the needs of all family members during the few hours of family time that remain each week. Moreover, improvements in medical care, automobile safety, housing, and consumer electronics have been remarkable, but they cannot be measured in a study such as this. Similarly, deterioration of the environment and an increase in crime rates cannot be quantified but may have high costs in terms of health, safety, and enjoyment. . . .

Baby Boomers in Retirement

Overall, CBO expects that baby boomers will have higher real retirement incomes than older people today for a variety of reasons.

• First, as long as real wage growth is positive, on average, during the next 20 years to 40 years, boomers will have higher real preretirement earnings than today's older people had in their working years. Under current law, this growth will increase the level of boomers' Social Security benefits. Pension benefits will be higher as well, and higher earnings now will enable them to save more for retirement.

• Second, increases in women's participation in the labor force imply that more boomers will have acquired more years of work experience before retirement. Not only will more women be eligible for their own Social Security and pension benefits, but also their income from these sources in some cases will be higher.

• Third, boomers will be more likely to receive income from pensions as a result of recent changes in the pension system.

• Finally, baby boomers may inherit substantial wealth from their parents.

Several caveats must accompany these optimistic findings. One of the most important assumptions leading to these results is that wages will grow more rapidly than prices during the next 40 years. Although most growth in real wages in the long run comes from technical progress, low saving and capital investment will reduce the growth of real wages. In addition, changes in government tax and benefit policies could affect these conclusions. Changes that increase taxes or reduce benefits could leave retirees with lower discretionary income. For example, during the next three or four decades, as the proportion of retirees in the population rises, Social Security taxes could be raised or benefits could be reduced. In addition, benefits and financing of Medicare may be altered as part of the effort to reduce the deficit and possibly as part of general health care reform.

Although the future looks bright for those who are well educated, it is somewhat gloomy for those with few marketable skills. The baby boomers are one of the most highly educated cohorts in history, with one of every four completing four years of college as of 1989. Those with a college education can expect higher incomes, faster wage growth, and more resources available for saving. However, the prospects of earning a decent wage are much poorer for those without skills valued by the marketplace. The job opportunities for those without a college education or technical skills will probably continue to shrink in the future as the workplace places a growing premium on advanced skills and training.

Marital Status and Homeownership

Marital status is also important in determining financial well-being both before and after retirement, especially for women. Being married today usually means having two incomes and sharing many expenses, with housing among the most significant. Fringe benefits, particularly health insurance coverage, are usually better for married couples than for single people because the gaps in one spouse's benefits are often filled by the other. These financial benefits continue in the retirement years, and under current law a significant percentage of wives also receive more generous Social Security payments based on their husband's work history rather than their own. Widows especially gain from their husband's more extensive work history.

Homeownership may be an important indicator of the potential for lifetime earnings and at least in the past has contributed to wealth through sizable capital gains on housing assets. Homeowners to date have accumulated significantly more wealth than nonhomeowners. Their wealth is in nonhousing assets as well as in housing, although this may reflect the relationship between income and wealth rather than between homeownership and wealth. If this continues to be true in the future, those who are unable to buy a home as young adults might be less financially well off in retirement than those who could afford to become homeowners. Although CBO cannot forecast whether housing will continue to be a good investment in the years to come, we have found that households headed by older people who own their homes tend to be financially better off in retirement.

Two implications emerge. The first is that single, poorly educated baby boomers may face a bleak economic future, depending heavily on public programs. The current cohort of retirees also faces this prospect. The second is that nonhomeowners may be unable to accumulate wealth at a rate that is sufficient to give them a comfortable lifestyle in retirement. Although most baby boomers will enjoy higher incomes and more wealth than their parents, some types of households will be struggling to make ends meet. . . .

Response to Criticisms of the CBO Study

Now let me deal with two criticisms of the CBO study. First, some people might argue that even if the saving behavior of baby boomers is comparable to that of their parents, this doesn't mean much since their parents didn't save adequately themselves but have benefited from fortuitous circumstances. Yet the evidence shows that the parents' generation was saving at a moderately high rate prior to the 1970s and 1980s. Only after receiving good news regarding Social Security benefits, housing capital gains, and Medicare expansion did they reduce their saving rates. Indeed, a [National Bureau of Economic Research] paper by Orazio P. Attanasio argues persuasively that the age-saving profile shifted downward for those aged 45–60 in the 1980s. Boomers are behaving the way their parents did *before* their elders learned about the windfalls from housing and Social Security, so it seems wrong to assume they will follow in their parents' footsteps the rest of the way toward retirement if we expect them to be confronted by different economic circumstances.

This line of reasoning reinforces the need for more information, education, and counseling in financial matters for boomers and for people of all ages. But recognizing that behavior does change in response to economic circumstances, both good and bad, is important.

Second, CBO has included housing wealth in the measure of household wealth, even though some research finds that older people do not wish to use housing equity to finance expenses in retirement. The relevant question, however, is not whether people desire to spend down their housing equity but whether policymakers should ignore it when evaluating the adequacy of resources to finance retirement living. CBO believes that policymakers should include housing in household wealth because households can use that wealth when needed. Indeed, recent research shows that households do in fact reduce housing equity in the year or two before death. At the very least, homeownership means more discretionary income in retirement since the household need not pay rent and most older households have paid off the mortgage. And baby boomers are likely to find innovative ways to tap their home equity without moving, perhaps through reverse mortgages, home equity loans, or some new kind of loan.

Finally, the CBO study does not address the likelihood that baby boomers will pay higher tax rates or receive reduced benefits in the future as this country faces up to its fiscal problems. Without a doubt, policymakers will have to pay more attention to resolving fiscal imbalances projected for the future. As illustrated by the proposal by [former] Rep. Dan Rostenkowski (D-IL) to shore up the finances of Social Security, policymakers recognize that changes must be made soon to avoid more severe cuts in later years.

Encouraging Signs

It is much too early to predict the financial circumstances of baby boomers in retirement with any accuracy. Nevertheless, for the average boomer, the early signs are moderately encouraging. As long as the economy continues to grow so that real incomes continue to rise, public and private pension systems remain intact, and health care costs do not explode, baby boomers should enjoy higher real incomes in retirement than their parents' generation currently does. But for some, as discussed above, the outlook is considerably worse.

"The number with the disease is expected to grow exponentially, with as many as 14 million by the year 2050."

More Elderly People May Develop Alzheimer's Disease

Robin Marantz Henig

Alzheimer's is a progressive degenerative disease that causes premature senility among many older people. In the following viewpoint, Robin Marantz Henig argues that diagnosis of Alzheimer's has risen significantly and that the ailment has become the fourth-leading cause of death in America. Henig maintains that the incidence of Alzheimer's, which afflicts four million people, increases exponentially with age, beginning with those in their sixties, and is most pervasive among the elderly over eighty-five, a population that is growing rapidly. Henig is the author of *The Myth of Senility* and is a frequent contributor to the *New York Times Magazine*.

As you read, consider the following questions:

1. What is sometimes mistaken for Alzheimer's, according to Henig?
2. Why is Alzheimer's difficult to diagnose with certainty, according to the author?
3. According to Henig, what personality changes may Alzheimer's induce?

In little more than a decade, Alzheimer's disease has moved from an obscure and supposedly rare condition to become the nation's fourth-leading cause of death. The disease slowly but relentlessly eviscerates a lifetime of memories, destroying brain cells and blocking communication from one cell to another. It eventually erases all that makes a person alive, unique and human. A Gallup Poll found that one of every three Americans now knows someone who has it and that nearly 50 percent worry about developing it themselves. The disease afflicts four million people, and family after family has a sad story to tell about it.

Harriet H., for example, says she did not understand her husband's condition until the night they gave a dinner party at their suburban Washington home. "It was a very nice evening; we all had a wonderful time," she says. "And then as people were getting ready to leave, my husband put on his coat to leave with them. He didn't know he was in his own home."

Diagnosing Alzheimer's

In part because of the increased familiarity with the ailment, there is concern in the medical world that people, and occasionally their doctors, are jumping too quickly to a diagnosis of Alzheimer's disease when all that's happening is normal aging. Scientists now recognize that Alzheimer's is totally different from the memory lapses that plague everyone who gets old; it is a specific, organic condition that develops only in some human brains.

"There is some tendency to diagnose Alzheimer's disease too readily when one is presented with the everyday kind of forgetfulness that all of us have," says Leonard Berg, professor of neurology at Washington University School of Medicine in St. Louis and chairman of the medical and scientific board of the Alzheimer's Association. "Alzheimer's disease is the new phrase on the block."

Being too quick to the diagnosis can be tragic. In making such a judgment, the doctor might be overlooking some physical and potentially treatable condition that can cause almost identical symptoms. What looks like Alzheimer's might, in fact, be caused by one of scores of underlying, often treatable, conditions—including depression, drug intoxication, thyroid imbalance, vitamin B-12 deficiency, even a mild heart attack.

The first step when evaluating an elderly patient complaining of memory loss is "to do a neurologic exam to see if the patient really has dementia," says Daniel A. Pollen, a neurologist at the University of Massachusetts. Dementia is the loss of intellectual abilities, like memory, judgment and language, without a loss of consciousness or alertness. "Then, if there is dementia, you have to look for a treatable cause that might explain it," adds

Pollen, the author of *Hannah's Heirs: The Quest for the Genetic Origins of Alzheimer's Disease*. A thorough examination is the only way to rule out these possibilities.

Discovery of Alzheimer's

The disease is named after Alois Alzheimer, a German psychiatrist who in 1907 reported the perplexing case of a 51-year-old woman who experienced intellectual deterioration. When his patient died, incontinent and bedridden, four years later, Alzheimer conducted an autopsy of her brain. He found it riddled with two abnormal cell formations that he characterized as "plaques" and "tangles." These two types of brain cell masses are today the hallmarks of the neurological disease that bears his name.

Subsequent research has shown that the plaques are made of a brain protein known as beta-amyloid and that the tangles consist of abnormal nerve cell filaments wrapped around each other like a fraying piece of twine. To this day, the only way that Alzheimer's disease can be diagnosed with absolute certainty is if brain tissue examined under a microscope, usually after death, turns up sufficient evidence of these tangles and plaques. Brain biopsies are rarely done because they are difficult and dangerous.

Looking at Alzheimer's

The brains of Alzheimer's victims have two physical characteristics that distinguish them from those of the normal elderly: dense deposits of proteins not usually found in the brain, and tangles of twisted nerve cell fibers. Those abnormalities collect in the hippocampus—the area of the brain where new information is turned into memory—and in parts of the cerebral cortex responsible for language and other cognitive functions.

What went wrong? Alzheimer's is probably several diseases with similar results. Researchers are focusing on genes that seem to malfunction and overproduce or misdirect the enemy proteins.

Lee Smith, *Fortune*, April 17, 1995.

For many years, the diagnosis of Alzheimer's disease was used only for early-onset, then called "presenile," dementia. "When I went to medical school in the 40's, we were taught that Alzheimer's disease was a very rare disorder affecting people in their 40's and 50's and that none of us was ever going to see a case in our lifetimes," Berg says. "They told us that something else happens to old people, but because it affected people in their 60's and 70's, they weren't going to go into that."

Gradually, though, scientists realized that the same plaques and tangles that appeared in the brains of people who died of presenile dementia were found in the brains of people with a later onset of the very same symptoms. Since the late 1970's, Alzheimer's disease has been used to mean dementia caused by a specific kind of brain degeneration no matter what the age of the patient.

Pinpointing Alzheimer's

In much of medicine, the diagnosis of a specific disease is made by ruling out others. This is true of Alzheimer's. "If you have a good history of progression over a year or more, and if you've ruled out the possible reversible causes of the symptoms, you can usually make a diagnosis of Alzheimer's disease," Pollen says. "Some people like to do MRI [magnetic resonance imaging] or CT [computerized tomography] scans to see whether there's brain atrophy —but these are only consistent with the diagnosis, not proof."

Reversible pseudo-dementia occurs in only about 10 percent of patients who come in for evaluations. Still, it's worth looking for, since the alternative is to consign someone with a treatable disease to a category of illness that's progressive and incurable.

Just as there are reports of overdiagnosis, so too are there reports of underdiagnosis. Some physicians are reluctant to give such a dire name to a patient's condition; instead, they say the forgetfulness and confusion are the inevitable result of aging. "A patient came to us just a few weeks ago with dementia, who had been told by his doctor that it's just normal aging, and there's nothing anyone can do," Pollen says. It may not prove to be either; it's possible that something can be done or that it's not normal aging at all but rather a case of Alzheimer's.

A Growing At-Risk Population

Overdiagnosis does not completely explain why Alzheimer's seems so common today, affecting a million more Americans than a decade ago. A fuller explanation is the population growth of the people at highest risk. Alzheimer's is overwhelmingly a disease of very old age. Those over 85 represent the fastest-growing segment of the population. As this age group expands, the number with the disease is expected to grow exponentially, with as many as 14 million by the year 2050.

The prevalence rates rise steeply with age, according to a 1989 study conducted in the working-class neighborhood of East Boston. "We went door to door and interviewed everyone over 65," says Dr. Denis A. Evans, who coordinated the study while at the Brigham and Women's Hospital in Boston. More than 3,800 older people were interviewed and 467 were asked to come to a health center for further evaluations. From this sample, Evans's group concluded that for people aged 65 to 74, the prevalence of Alzheimer's was 3 percent; for those aged 75 to 84, it was 19 percent, and for people over the age of 85, the rate of Alzheimer's disease was an astonishing 47 percent. Earlier estimates had put the rate at closer to 20 to 30 percent.

"The age distribution curve," says Evans, now at Rush-Presbyterian–St. Luke's Medical Center in Chicago, "implies a dramatic increase in prevalence of the illness in the years ahead." The economic implications are staggering. The four million who have the disease now cost the nation some $90 billion a year. "Imagine the whole state of Texas," says Zaven S. Khachaturian, associate director of the National Institute on Aging. "Imagine all those people in need of long-term nursing home care. Our society simply cannot afford it."

Genetic Markers

In response to the problem, Federal support for Alzheimer's research has increased tenfold since 1983. This has led to an eruption of scientific discoveries in the past few years. Biologists have now identified several genetic markers that seem to correlate with early-onset Alzheimer's disease, which affects as many as 10 percent of Alzheimer's patients.

For the past 15 years, researchers have focused on the plaques and tangles identified by Alzheimer back in 1907. These brain abnormalities are most plentiful in two critical regions of the brain: the hippocampus, which controls memory, and the cerebral cortex, which controls higher order thinking and reasoning.

In those same regions, you can also find high concentrations of beta-amyloid, the protein in many of the plaques. This finding led to the amyloid hypothesis: that the first step in a sequence of destructive events in the brain involves beta-amyloid. But a small group of Alzheimer's researchers have questioned the amyloid hypothesis, saying the presence of beta-amyloid in Alzheimer's brains is the result, rather than the cause, of the brain cell devastation.

Then in 1993, scientists at Duke University made one of the most important discoveries since Alois Alzheimer's original finding. They linked a different gene to an increased susceptibility to the most common form of Alzheimer's, the form that strikes after the age of 65.

The Duke scientists, led by Allen D. Roses, a neurobiologist, offered an alternative to the amyloid hypothesis. They proposed that the first step in the brain cell degeneration involves a protein called apolipoprotein E (ApoE).

The scientists found that 64 percent of Alzheimer's patients had at least one gene coding for the type of the ApoE protein known as E4. Among a control group, only 31 percent did. And they charted a clear relationship between the ApoE types and the age of onset of the disease. For those Alzheimer's patients with two E4 genes, one from each parent, the average age of onset was 68. For those with a single E4, paired with another type like E3, the average age was 75. For those with no E4, the average age of onset was 84.

It became clear, then, that having ApoE4 is a risk factor for Alzheimer's disease, just as high cholesterol is a risk factor for heart disease. "If you have E4, you're more likely to get Alzheimer's disease; if you don't have E4, you're less likely," Roses says. Research on how E4 works, he says, holds promise for a preventive therapy year 2004, perhaps as simple as a pill to supply a missing brain chemical.

Just as diet and exercise can lessen the risk of heart disease for someone with high cholesterol, something in the environment might affect whether a person with E4 actually develops Alzheimer's. So far, evidence of environmental influences on Alzheimer's disease is scanty. But two studies have raised some possibilities.

Other Signs

At the University of Southern California in Los Angeles, Dr. Victor Henderson reviewed the medical records and death certificates of some 2,400 women who had lived in Southern California and found that those who had been on estrogen replacement therapy were 40 percent less likely to have had Alzheimer's than those who had not taken estrogen. And at Duke, John Breitner examined 50 pairs of elderly twins who developed Alzheimer's disease at different ages—or in which only one twin ever developed the disease—and found that those who took anti-inflammatory drugs for arthritis were four times more likely than their co-twins to have developed Alzheimer's at a later age, or to be spared altogether. Now clinical trials are under way to see whether estrogen replacement therapy or anti-inflammatory drugs offer protection against Alzheimer's.

Alzheimer's Symptoms

When the brain cell destruction begins, the effect is at first insidious. The earliest symptoms of the disease—often noticeable only in retrospect—are loss of recent memory and impaired judgment. But often these deficits are easily disguised. "My husband maintained his poise for a very long time," says Harriet H., whose husband's diagnosis in 1982 came after signs of decline that began eight years before. "If we ran into you on the

119

street and you were a friend, he would say: 'How are you? Nice to see you. How's your family?' And you would think he was absolutely fine. But he would have no idea who you were. If you were a stranger from New Guinea who had just set foot on our shores, he would say the same thing."

At first, it's hard to distinguish these symptoms from normal forgetfulness. Harriet's husband, for instance, had always been absent-minded. But as the brain decays, the memory loss becomes more profound; people forget not only where they left their glasses but that they ever wore glasses. As the brain deteriorates, Alzheimer's changes not only memory but personality. One patient may lash out at a spouse or child; another, retreat into silence, or become confused, paranoid or belligerent. In the final stages, usually about 8 to 10 years after diagnosis, patients are often unable to control their bodily functioning, becoming unable to speak, swallow or recognize their own families.

Harriet cared for her husband at home for 10 years. Finally, when he could no longer walk and barely recognized anyone, she put him in a nursing home. Since there is no cure, this is where most Alzheimer's patients spend their last years—bedridden, incontinent, an empty, sad shell of what they once were.

Curiously, the body often stays intact while the mind falls to pieces. Harriet is still moved to tears by her husband's face, which looks younger than its 80 years. "He's always had a very sweet face. Now it's just the same sweet face, but it's lost all its tension." Despite his mute helplessness, she can recognize in that face the man she once loved, the man who, in a changed but no less powerful way, she loves still. "It's a very dear face. He's a very dear man."

"I see the possibility of having a very good old age."

The Elderly Can Enjoy a Healthy Old Age

George Leonard

Old age can be a period of physical and mental excellence, George Leonard argues in the following viewpoint. Leonard describes his transformation from a nonathletic youth to an older adult who began to pursue many physical activities. Leonard, a martial arts expert, is a contributing editor for *Esquire* magazine and the author of *Education and Ecstasy, The Ultimate Athlete,* and *Mastery.*

As you read, consider the following questions:

1. How does young age compare with old age, according to Leonard?
2. How did Leonard demonstrate his coordination skills to an exercise physiologist?
3. What does the author mean by "turning off the chatter"?

I tend not to think about the fact that I'm getting older until people bring it to my attention. I'm sixty-seven, but I really don't feel that old. The truth of the matter is I feel just the same. One of my mentors was Dan Mish, the editor-in-chief of *Look*. Someone said he had the appearance of a Renaissance archbishop and wielded approximately the same power. Anyway, I was over at his house and after a few drinks I said, "You know, Dan, you just turned sixty." He said, "When you get up here it feels just the same. It's just the same." You know, when you're young you look at an old person and say, "Well, it must be very different." But it's not different; it's just the same. You see a good-looking woman, you have that same feeling. You see a football game, you ask yourself, Why couldn't I run out and catch that pass? I still do a lot of exercise, I still play a crazy game of frisbee, and I practice aikido daily. I know intellectually that I'm aging, but it doesn't feel that different. Everything seems about the same. . . .

A Late Bloomer

When I was twenty or so back in the 1940s I was interested in swing music. I had a thirteen-piece swing band, and we played Benny Goodman and Count Basie arrangements, and it was the biggest thrill in my life. I never achieved that kind of glory since and I never will again—to have a very successful big band and play at all the dances in your hometown, and even tour. But I was absolutely unathletic. I was a skinny kid, you know. And at that time skinny was considered disgraceful. In the 1930s, muscle tone wasn't even considered. Look back at old *Life* magazines—they have all these beefcake pictures of lifeguards, and all of them were fat—so I really was kind of an outsider. I never got into sports until in my forties. I'm one of those late-blooming jocks. I started aikido at age forty-seven, then got into the running craze when I was fifty. If I'd been running at twenty, God knows how fast I'd be running now, but I wasn't running at twenty. So the truth of the matter is that I could run faster at age fifty than I could at age twenty.

Just yesterday I was with a group of aging people, and we were with a young exercise physiologist who had created an exercise program for us. One of the things she had us do was hit a ball against a wall. She said, "This is very important, because as we get older we lose our hand-eye coordination." I was about to say something, but I kept my mouth shut. So then she has us jump up and down for a while and stand on one foot for ten seconds. "This is important," she said, "because as we grow older our sense of balance begins to fall off." And I said, "Wait, hold it, hold it. Our sense of balance might fall off. Our hand-eye coordination might fall off. But they might also improve." She was all flustered. I said, "Don't do us any more favors. This is ageism, and I will fight it on every front." So I said, "Okay, let's do some coordination things. How old are you?" "Twenty," she says. "I'm sixty-seven," I said, "and my reflex is obviously much slower than yours. Obviously my synaptic connections are not going to be as good as yours." I'm getting her kind of scared, you know? Then I said, "Let's do this game." And I got her doing this hand-slapping reaction game, and she couldn't even touch me. We also played this little game of pushing each other off balance. I was clobbering her all over the place.

The point I went on to make to this young woman is this: If at age twenty I was operating at 80 percent of my potential, and then at age sixty I was operating at 80 percent of my potential, obviously the twenty-year-old would win. But how many of us are working at 80 percent of our potential at age twenty? Very few—a tiny, tiny percentage. So the possibility exists that if I start training myself at age forty-seven in aikido, and now, at sixty-seven, I'm operating at 80 percent of my potential, in balance and coordination I'm a lot better than I was at age twenty when I only operated at 10 percent of my potential. When you see things in this light, you can improve at any age.

Viv Quillan for the *New Internationalist*. Reprinted with permission.

Unlike so many people, I don't see the spiritual as disconnected from the body. One of the great mistakes of the great religious traditions is that all of them have denigrated the body as being mere flesh, all evil, a gift of Satan. Our job is to get as far away as possible from the body to achieve enlightenment. I think that's a mistake. Modern physics shows us that matter is just another form of energy—a very compacted, relatively stable form of energy. So one of the most encouraging things for me has been the growth of the participatory sports movement in the United States. I think we must change our attitude toward the body, and our attitude toward aging. Like my wife now; she achieved a black belt in aikido, but as a kid she lay around and read books, literature and philosophy. She never ran at all. Now she says, "Come on out, show me how to catch a ball so we can play better." We have gloves and bats and softballs, all sorts of sports equipment. And she does aerobics and her coordination's gotten much better. At first she couldn't throw a frisbee, but now she really whips it out there. She's a much better athlete now than she was at age twenty, much better. Of course, as you get older you sometimes run into arthritis, things like that, and then you're necessarily limited. But whatever the limits are you can always do a little more than you think you can, and you can get a certain pleasure out of that. I think a big part of the whole aging story is staying in shape. . . .

Mental and Spiritual Health

I've had a chance to look at aging in America because my mother lives in a retirement community. I see that people who didn't have many resources, who were not very interested in life when they were younger, become miserable rather quickly. I've noticed that as you get older you desperately need other people, friends and so forth. If you're preoccupied with yourself, you've had it—the whole universe will become yourself. The universe will become your pains and aches and your complaints, and when the universe becomes your complaint, then it's not a very nice place to live in.

I think it's important to stay interested, to stay vitally interested in world affairs; to have some religious interest is very important; to have interest in other people; to have a community of people with whom you really share things, not superficially, but with whom you share your worries as well as your triumphs. I see the possibility of having a very good old age.

I suppose it's all a matter of desire. I certainly would like to recommend things that involve the body, if possible—some of the old favorites like yoga, t'ai chi, things that have a meditative aspect in them, because then you do tend to get the spiritual. And the spiritual is simply turning off the chatter. I'm not particularly interested in what god or what religion you follow, so long as you can get that focus or concentration and leave off the eternal chatter of daily life. Then the world rolls right into you, the world and all of its glory rolls right into you—and that's the wonder of existence.

==
"Public policy can and must take seriously a variety of different ideas about a good old age."
==

Quality of Life for the Elderly: Four Scenarios

Harry R. Moody

In the following viewpoint, Harry R. Moody presents four scenarios and case examples on the future quality of life for the elderly. The scenarios consider possibilities that include a longer period of deteriorating quality of life, the postponement of illness later into life, an increase in maximum life expectancy, and the allocation of health care with future generations in mind. Moody contends that questions about the meaning of old age and future policies affecting quality of life for the elderly should be discussed now. Moody is the acting director of the Brookdale Center on Aging of Hunter College in New York City.

As you read, consider the following questions:

1. In Moody's first scenario, why does Mr. Y decide not to have his pacemaker recharged?
2. What should health care resources be directed toward, according to the author's third scenario?
3. What does Moody compare longevity with in the fourth scenario?

Harry R. Moody, "Four Scenarios for an Aging Society," *Hastings Center Report*, vol. 24, no. 5, September/October 1994. Reprinted by permission of the author and the Hastings Center.

In *Gulliver's Travels* Jonathan Swift gives a portrait of the Struldbruggs, a race condemned to immortality without the blessing of good health: "They were the most mortifying sight I ever beheld. . . . Besides the usual deformities in extreme old age, they acquired an additional ghastliness in proportion to their number of years, which is not to be described."

Do the Struldbruggs conjure up a gloomy image of our own future? There is reason to think so. Modern health care permits growing numbers of people to live to advanced age under circumstances that call into question the meaning of continued survival. Yet some answers to questions about the meaning of survival are indispensable as we ponder how much it is worth spending on geriatric health care.

But can we talk coherently about meaning? No topic seems less promising for public debate than the "meaning of life." In advanced industrialized societies, public silence about the ultimate ends of life has become a ruling dogma. The problem, if anything, is even more troubling when we try to think about the meaning of the last stage of life. Chronological age by itself no longer carries an agreed-upon set of meanings for people at any point in life. The coming of an "age-irrelevant society" means loss of consensus about the values appropriate for different stages of life, including the last stage. It is no longer possible to say what a "rational person" of advanced years might prefer concerning medical treatment to prolong life, especially if the conditions for survival are drastically different from conditions that previously gave meaning or purpose to life.

As the aging population itself becomes more diverse, we confront ethical dilemmas raised by cost-containment, self-determined death, and biomedical technologies to postpone aging. Without confronting questions about the meaning of old age, we risk impoverishing discussion of public allocation choices that we must face. Perhaps the best we can do is to frame the issues clearly in terms of contrasting ideas about "meaning" and examine what resource allocation policies might follow from those contrasts. What follows are four scenarios about the future of an aging society, each based on plausible extrapolations from present empirical trends along with assumptions about the meaning of old age.

1. Prolongation of Morbidity

How shall we escape the prospect of joining the Struldbruggs? How do we avoid burgeoning numbers of demented but healthy Struldbruggs whose caregiving cost could bankrupt the health care system? The first scenario to be considered takes its point of departure from recent debates about the so-called compression of morbidity or postponement of sickness in later life. Recent data suggest that life expectancy among the aged has risen.

But the paradoxical result is longer periods of both health and sickness among different subgroups of elderly. The young-old (ages 65–75) tend to be healthier, but more and more of the old-old (75+) face decrepitude.

Outlook for the 85-Plus Elderly

Over 4,000,000 elderly persons need assistance with one or more everyday activities. Chronic illnesses increase with age and are more common among women, who average more years of chronic illness than men. Among those aged 85 and over, almost 25% live in a nursing home because of serious health problems. Of the oldest elderly living at home, about 20% are unable to carry on a major activity and 40% have a condition that limits their activities. Functional limitations are highest among elderly black women and those with relatively low incomes.

It is possible to get a rough idea of the need for family support over time by looking at the relative sizes of the population 85 years and over, compared with the number aged 50–64 years. In 1950, there were three people 85 years and older per 100 aged 50–64. In 1990, there were nine. That ratio will at least triple again to 28 by 2050.

Cynthia M. Taeuber, *USA Today*, September 1993.

What will the future bring? Under a pessimistic assumption, the period of morbidity will grow longer. Even modest medical technology—for example, antibiotics for Alzheimer patients—permits survival to advanced ages for those with very poor quality of life. If the meaning of old age is defined by the quality of life, then allocation policies should favor easing termination of treatment as a means of saving money. The quality-of-life standard could apply to all age groups, but prolongation of morbidity among the elderly means that this group would bear the brunt of cost-containment. The choice of death could be made either by individuals or by society, though the two levels are always intertwined, as the following case reveals.

Mr. Y's Decision

Case Example. Mr. Y, aged eighty-five, has long had a pacemaker and has been on a downhill course from Parkinson disease in recent years. Even with help, his wife can no longer care for him at home, but both reject the idea of entering a nursing home. Mr. Y has decided not to have his pacemaker recharged: he prefers to "go quickly" from heart failure rather than face the deteriorating quality of life he would have living in a nursing home.

A key element in his decision is the fact that, to qualify for Medicaid coverage of nursing home care, Mr. Y would have to spend down most of the couple's accumulated assets of $300,000. He prefers a life at home as long as he can remain, with peace of mind from knowing that his wife is well provided for after his death and that he can leave some legacy to his grandchildren.

Mr. Y's private decision is a reasonable one, though some will feel that it is cruel that he should have to choose death to preserve assets for his family. Others will feel that the quality-of-life standard adopted by Mr. Y as an individual should be extrapolated more generally as a matter of public policy. On grounds of justice if not of utility, perhaps we would redirect scarce resources toward those with a more favorable quality of life. Consistent with such a policy, we would adopt a permissive attitude toward all forms of self-determined death, including active euthanasia and assisted suicide. The problem with this strategy is that a merely permissive attitude toward self-determined death may not actually save much money. In that case, those who favor reliance on a quality-of-life standard, for the aged or other groups, would have to move to harsher methods of rationing health care.

2. Compression of Morbidity

Perhaps the first scenario is too pessimistic. If we adopt a more optimistic assumption about compression of morbidity, then we should do everything possible to postpone illness later and later into life. The strategy here recalls Oliver Wendell Holmes's poem, "The Wonderful One-Horse Shay." That marvelous carriage was built so that every part of it "aged" at the same rate until, all at once, the whole thing fell apart together after a hundred years and a day.

This second scenario is based on a biological assumption that the maximum human life span is fixed at around 120 years. While we may not be able to surpass the limit, our goal should be to eliminate the signs and symptoms of age that appear before we arrive at it. The proper aim of medicine and public policy, therefore, would be to intervene, to slow down the rate of aging so that more and more of us can remain healthy up to the very end of life. Sickness or morbidity would be compressed into the last few months or weeks of life. At the end, the body would simply fall apart all at once, like the wonderful one-horse shay.

This second scenario assumes a fixed limit to life; within that limit, it aims for the modernization of old age, implicit in slogans like "successful aging" or "productive aging." Under this scenario allocation policies would favor medical research and health promotion to delay morbidity and make of old age an extension of middle age. The meaning of old age lies simply in an extension of the values of youth and middle age, and specific consequences follow for allocation of resources.

Case Example. The National Institute on Stroke is in a position to receive an increase in funding, but two factions within the institute are arguing about where the new money should go. One group favors investment in clinical research on promising rehabilitation methods for severely impaired stroke patients. The other group favors an outreach campaign of hypertension screening tied to health education to reduce the likelihood of stroke or postpone it for some substantial number of people. The rehabilitation advocates believe those who are sickest deserve our attention, while the hypertension screening group believes in a compression-of-morbidity strategy.

3. Prolongevity

The third scenario pushes the modern idea of progress still further by challenging the "natural" limits presumed under the second scenario. If 120 years of life is good, why isn't 150 years better? Why not try to raise the maximum life span of the species? Instead of the idea of "normal" aging, we should think of aging as a disease to be conquered and cured. According to this third scenario, the entire human life course is open to revision by new knowledge of the biology of aging, especially the genetics of longevity. According to this scenario scarce health care resources should not be expended on incremental gains in life expectancy or improving quality of life but should rather be directed toward basic research into the aging process itself. For example, perhaps gene therapy will provide a breakthrough permitting us to raise maximum life span. The ultimate goal is indefinite survival under favorable conditions of technological control. The meaning of aging as we have known it through human history would change radically. Aging would be progressively postponed and eventually eliminated.

Case Example. The National Institute on Aging [NIA] is setting aside funds for young investigators involved in basic research. One group of new applications involves genetic markers linked to Alzheimer disease, while the other involves studies of genetic and environmental factors that can raise maximum life span in animal populations such as fruit flies, nematodes, and fish. The charter of the NIA specifically indicates that its mission is to "add life to years" rather than seeking to raise maximum life span. Supporters of "prolongevity" appeal to the work of investigators like Roy Walford and Michael Rose, suggesting we may be on the point of a breakthrough that could raise the maximum human life span from 120 years to 150 years or more. Supporters of the NIA's traditional agenda believe that this new knowledge is not worth pursuing at the expense of the traditional goal of quality aging. Some argue more darkly that a prolongevity strategy poses risky moral dilemmas for society.

4. Recovery of the Life World

The fourth scenario assumes that the meaning of old age lies in the finitude of human life as a condition to be voluntarily accepted as a matter of collective policy, not individual choice. This strategy rejects the "biomedicalization of old age" in favor of what Jürgen Habermas calls the life world. In effect, the fourth strategy seeks intentionally to recapture some of the virtues of the traditional idea of "stages of life." More broadly, the fourth scenario evokes an ideal of vital involvement and concern by the elderly for the welfare of future generations. This fourth scenario can be understood by analogy with the environmental movement: longevity, we might argue, just like economic growth, can reasonably be restricted for reasons of solidarity or intergenerational justice. The common good and the needs of future generations are values that support limiting longevity in any one generation. Allocation policies for health care would embody these values by favoring social programs such as hospice or home health care as against high-tech medical interventions that provide only incremental gains for those who already have lived a long and full life, as the following case illustrates.

Case Example. The administrator of the Health Care Financing Administration (HCFA) is under pressure to contain Medicare costs while at the same time expanding services. He is considering whether Medicare should reimburse the cost of a new class of experimental cancer drugs under a "compassionate protocol" procedure, which would likely increase demand for the drug from many elderly patients. For the same amount of money HCFA could liberalize reimbursement rules to provide stimulus for community long-term care services such as geriatric day care, respite, and hospice programs. Some voices within the agency argue that the drug expenditures would help the least advantaged (those who are sickest), while others argue that community-based long-term services will both help more people and provide care for people from all age groups.

Weighing the Four Scenarios

The first scenario, prolongation of morbidity, poses a dilemma for the goals of medicine. Should medicine strive to prevent death or to eliminate suffering? What if achieving the first frustrates the second, and vice versa? The irony is that it is the "success" of medicine that leads to its "failure": a meaningless life, prolonged for no purpose, as in the case of the Struldbruggs— another instance of the law of unintended consequences repeated so often in the history of technology.

The second scenario, the compression of morbidity, only achieves its goal if it is possible to postpone *every* disease or chronic condition until just before death. Like the Star Wars [missile defense] program, the strategy assumes we can eliminate accidents. But the effort is defeated by chance, by the inability to achieve total control, since it is improbable that all systems of the organism will wear out simultaneously.

The third scenario, prolongevity, confronts the same problem. What if something goes wrong earlier in life—not just in youth or middle age, but, say, at age sixty or seventy? "Something going wrong" is another name for accidents, which are bound to kill in the end. The genetic potential for higher maximum life span overall is no guarantee against incurring accidental insults along the way. We escape the law of fate only to succumb to the law of chance.

Furthermore, if prolongevity were successful it would pose other social problems. Longer life means greater diversity, which is another name for inequality. Life span extension would intensify all such inequalities and give rise to envy on the part of those who have less. The result would probably be a weakening of the will for collective provision. For instance, why should minority groups with lower average life expectancy pay taxes for dominant groups who could expect lives of a century or more?

Serious equity problems would also arise if the fourth scenario were adopted. Even under collective spending limits, individuals concerned about health promotion could aim for compression of morbidity, while biomedical research might at any time open up unexpected possibilities for extending the life span. Both strategies are attractive to wealthier, better educated groups in society. The inequalities of life expectancy would again be difficult to control, particularly in a period when welfare states impose tighter cost controls on the collective provision of health care. The result would be to raise longevity selectively, making inequities even more severe.

The Political Question

Under conditions of increased longevity and new medical technology, old age no longer carries a fixed meaning. Instead, alternative meanings such as quality of life, successful aging, indefinite survival, and collective acceptance of limits each entail very different consequences for the allocation of scarce resources. This plurality of meanings will not be eliminated by appealing to a "natural" life course nor by Rawlsian arguments that separate the right from the good. On the contrary, public policy can and must take seriously a variety of different ideas about a good old age.

My purpose here has not been to advance any single idea about the meaning of old age. Rather it is to highlight the way in which different allocation choices presuppose very specific ideas about the meaning of the last stage of life. Certain ideas about meaning and value—for example, quality of life, successful aging, or intergenerational solidarity—are intrinsically problematic because they involve difficult philosophical questions about the purpose of human life and especially the last stage of life. Both technocratic discourse and an exclusively procedural theory of justice try to evade these hard choices but will find that questions about the meaning of old age come back to haunt us in the end. Perhaps it is better to wrestle with these demons right now.

Periodical Bibliography

The following articles have been selected to supplement the diverse views presented in this chapter. Addresses are provided for periodicals not indexed in the *Readers' Guide to Periodical Literature*, the *Alternative Press Index*, or the *Social Sciences Index*.

American Behavioral Scientist	Special issue: "Aging Well in Contemporary Society, Part I," November/December 1995. Available from Sage Publications, 2455 Teller Rd., Thousand Oaks, CA 91320.
Christopher Byron	"The Boomers Go Bust," *Esquire*, July 1995.
Jack Challem	"Keeping Your Marbles," *Natural Health*, January/February 1995.
Marilyn Chase	"The Baby Boom Hits Fifty," *Wall Street Journal*, October 31 and November 1–2, 1995.
Lindley H. Clark Jr.	"A Dandy Retirement, If You Can Pay," *Wall Street Journal*, May 25, 1994.
Betty Friedan	"Beyond the Age Mystique," *In Context*, Winter 1993/1994.
Ellen Graham	"What It Was Like to Be Fifty in '50," *Wall Street Journal*, November 2, 1995.
Gerald F. Kreyche	"Retirement: Enjoying Life in the Fast Lane," *USA Today*, May 1993.
Richard Laliberte	"Body Aging? You Don't Have to Give In," *New Choices for Retirement Living*, July/August 1995.
Janet Novack	"Making the Golden Years Golden," *Forbes*, January 16, 1995.
Spencer Rich	"Will Boomers Go Bust?" *Washington Post National Weekly Edition*, July 17–23, 1995. Available from Reprints, 1150 15th St. NW, Washington, DC 20071.
Gail Sheehy	"New Passages," *U.S. News & World Report*, June 12, 1995.
Lee Smith	"Memory: Why You're Losing It, How to Save It," *Fortune*, April 17, 1995.
Ellyn E. Spragins	"Beyond Retirement," *Newsweek*, November 20, 1995.
Louis Uchitelle	"Retirement's Worried Face," *New York Times*, July 30, 1995.
USA Today	"Aging Population Faces the Future," April 1994.
Dan Wakefield	"Be Old Now," *Yoga Journal*, October 1995. Available from 2054 University Ave., Berkeley, CA 94704.

What Type of Health Care Should the Elderly Receive?

Chapter Preface

In the United States, more than 7 million elderly persons require long-term treatment for heart problems, strokes, cancer, and other illnesses and diseases. That number is expected to almost double by the year 2030.

Traditionally, such patients have received long-term care in hospitals or nursing homes. However, due to the high cost of institutional care and to seniors' desire to be cared for in their own homes or in community-based facilities, alternative types of care are growing in popularity.

For example, more patients than ever before now receive in-home care from professional live-in or visiting aides. According to *New York Times* writer Milt Freudenheim, "Home health care has been the fastest-growing segment of the fast-growing health care industry." Indeed, the number of seniors receiving Medicare (the largest payer of home care services) more than doubled from 1.6 million to 3.5 million between 1985 and 1995.

The effects of this trend on health care and on seniors appear to be mixed. Companies that provide home services point out that typical daily expenses are approximately one-tenth of the average $900-per-day hospital stay. But according to a federal audit of home health agencies in Florida, one in four claims to Medicare were either fraudulent or were charging for unnecessary services. As for the elderly themselves, while recipients pay lower health care costs and enjoy the familiar surroundings of home, many patients are dependent on unlicensed, inadequately trained, or unscreened care aides.

According to many observers, the high cost of health care, the doubling of the elderly population requiring long-term care, and seniors' desire to be treated in their own homes and communities demand a system that emphasizes proper long-term home- and community-based care. The authors in this chapter examine the costs of, and options for, long-term care for the elderly.

"What I considered a 'last resort,' I now regard as the best decision I could have made."

Nursing Homes Are Beneficial

Lou L. Hartney

Lou L. Hartney is a freelance writer in Montrose, Colorado. In the following viewpoint, Hartney describes her traumatic decision to place her elderly mother in a nursing home after years of caring for her at home. Guilt-ridden and uncertain at first, Hartney came to believe that placing her mother in a nursing home was positive. Hartney's mother enjoyed the companionship and structured activities the home provided.

As you read, consider the following questions:

1. What circumstances caused the author to settle her mother in a nursing home?
2. What negative reactions did Hartney's mother have to the nursing home?
3. According to Hartney, how did the nursing home help her mother?

Lou L. Hartney, "My Mother's Keeper," *Family Therapy Networker*, September/October 1989. Reprinted with permission.

July 28, 1987: It is too late to turn back. I have set in motion events that are tumbling me along like a broken branch in flood-tide. I have run out of choices. I look at my 94-year-old mother. Her thin, hunched body is dwarfed amid a welter of crates, cartons of books, piles of possessions to go to the Salvation Army, and other stacks of worthless items too precious to leave behind. Her expression matches the disheveled room. She doesn't know it yet, but by this time next week, she will be in a nursing home in Colorado, a thousand miles from here, whatever life remains to her drastically changed. The cost of dying, particularly if one does it slowly, is prohibitive in California.

Growing Older

She is leaving kind neighbors who remember spirited bridge games in which she held her own. She now forgets their names and faces from one day to the next, but I will never stop being grateful to them for coming in to see her often in recent years, telling her over and over who they are, for including her in dinner invitations, even though they know the diapers she now wears don't always do all they are supposed to. Will we ever find people who will brighten her life like that again?

My God, what am I doing to her?

July 30, 1987: Although I feel drained and exhausted, sleep evades me for hours these nights. While I am turning endlessly, I find myself wishing she could go peacefully in her sleep before I have to do this. She is almost a stranger now, consumed by fear that I will leave her sight to go even as far as the washer in the garage. She watches anxiously from the doorway when I go to the mailbox. If I have a sitter come in when I shop for groceries, she is anxious and hurt; if I take her with me, I am frantic.

Parents in Nursing Homes

I recall her words a few years back about a lifelong friend whose son put her in a nursing home where she eventually died. "I could have told her that daughters are closer to their mothers," she said, as if that were her personal guarantee against such a thing happening to her.

Sleep, when it comes at last, is as filled with foreboding as my waking hours.

August 4, 1987: Nothing is going right. I am sick with fear. The house is sold. The new owners are moving in tomorrow. I expect to hear the sound of the moving van grinding to a stop in front of the house at any moment.

I try to reconstruct the reasoning that led me into this morass. In retrospect, it doesn't make any sense at all. I look at earlier journal entries: "I don't care about golden streets—what I want out of Heaven is not to have to clean the bathroom a dozen times a day!" and "When will I get time to work at my writing—if that day ever comes, there won't be an original thought left in my head." There are other entries made in anger that I'm ashamed to re-read. The most civilized comment I find is: "It's not her fault or mine that the 'golden years' are tarnished for us both."

The Essentials of Care

Suddenly, the former 10-hour days in my home office seem to be a haven of safety and security. Work deadlines allowed little time for worry, a blessing that had gone unrecognized until now. True, they also permitted time for only the essentials of care for my mother. I fixed her meals, kept her clean, somehow got my work out on time, had crashing headaches.

Am I ready to trade that for a burden of guilt?

August 6, 1987: It is done, or at least begun. Our flight to Colorado was not as difficult as I had feared. Friends are driving my car from California, so my daughter, Linda, who lives in the Colorado town we are going to meets us and takes us to a motel. Mom can't negotiate the stairs at Linda's home, and I can't bear to take her to the nursing home at the end of an exhausting day for her. She sleeps soundly. After breakfast at a nearby coffee shop this morning, I know the time has come to try to explain what is ahead. I force the words out, that I can no longer take care of her, that she will be living at a place called a "care center," that I will see her every day, that I love her as much as ever. "Can you understand?" I ask. Her answer is a qualified, "I'll try."

Humane Care

Much is written about inappropriate nursing home use, but policy should also consider *appropriate* nursing home use. Ironically, the greatest support to family caregivers in some cases might be the provision of high-quality, humane institutional programs so that families could stop giving care—without guilt—when their (direct) help outlives its humane purpose.

Rosalie Kane, quoted in *America*, January 31, 1987.

I am expecting tears, pleas, perhaps anger, but she is outwardly calm. I wonder if she realizes what I am saying, and by the time my daughter arrives to take us to the nursing home, my face is streaked with tears. Linda puts on a cheerful front, and I wonder how I could get through it without her.

An Inspection Trip

The administrator of the nursing home, Mary, comes out to the car and greets Mom with a cheery, "Hello, Emily!" I had met

Mary on an inspection trip months earlier and had been impressed by her obvious understanding and honesty. Some of the other nearby facilities we had investigated had a policy of asking family members to stay away at least three days after the patient's admission. "Let us take all the flak at first," they said. "Then, when you show up, she'll be glad to see you." I felt that three days without a familiar face would be shattering to her, so when Mary assured me I could be with her as much as I wished, I made my choice.

She is put alone in a twin-bedded room. I stay until bedtime that evening and am there early the next morning. I find her sitting on the other bed in her room, a puzzled look on her face. "What day is this?" she asks. I tell her it is Friday. Her next question is, "When are we going home?" I start to explain, but she cuts me off. "You say this is Sunday?"

September 1, 1987: She has been put in a room with 97-year-old Belle. When I walk in today, my mother points toward her new roommate in her chair by the window and says, "That old woman's as deaf as a post!" As I am trying to find the right words of apology, I realize that Belle is, indeed, extremely hard of hearing and has no notion of what has just been said.

I didn't appreciate my mother's sense of tact until it was gone.

September 15, 1987: She has been in the nursing home five weeks now. I am renting a house in the country, and when I walk to my car alone, I'm often dizzy with a feeling of freedom. She begs me daily to stay all night with her. I try to convince her that two people can't sleep in a single hospital bed and, besides, the people who run the care center wouldn't allow it. She brushes my answer aside with, "They wouldn't even notice!"

She has been given a short and simple haircut. I admit I'm relieved to be freed from home permanents, shampoos, and settings, but she looks like a frail elf with a too-small head.

Trying to Understand

Part of the time she thinks she's in a hotel; other days, she asks me if it's a hospital. Today, she says, "Maybe this is a nut house—maybe you put me here because I'm nuts!" But there's no anger in her voice, no hurt, no hint of feeling betrayed. I think she is simply trying to understand.

November 12, 1987: She has good days and bad days. Her disposition, as always, is sweet. But sometimes she doesn't know her great-grandchildren, and they visit frequently. She often says, "And who are these beautiful children?" Sometimes she says to me, "Is Lou coming out today?" I answer, "Mom, I'm Lou." "Oh, of course," she says.

It is snowing today, and tree branches sag under the weight. She says, "Isn't this unusual for California?"

November 27, 1987: Today is her 95th birthday. Linda, the children, and I take fried chicken, rolls, and apple pie, all her favorites, and reserve the Activities Room, a glassed-in portion of the dining area used for special occasions. Mom goes to her regular table while we are setting things up. When I go to get her, she holds onto Belle's wheelchair. "I don't want to go unless Belle comes too," she says. That's fine with us; we just hadn't thought of it in advance. The children help her open her gifts, and the occasion comes close to gaiety.

Lonely Residents

December 17, 1987: The Christmas festivities are getting me down. Various groups are singing and bringing handmade gifts for the residents at the center. I sit with Mom as the beautiful voices fill the dining area. The staff people, too, are even kinder and more cheerful than usual. I am touched by their evident sincerity. But I am on the verge of tears throughout the holiday observances, not for my mother particularly. I tell myself my grief is for the residents who are alone, without a friend or relative there. I look at the faces around us. Some eyes are empty, like the windows of abandoned houses. Some are sad; all are sober. I can sense the weight of memories in those which comprehend the season.

An Important Function

Sometimes there is tremendous guilt in committing a parent. It may be the feeling of, my mother never sent me away, I was never too much for her, but she was too much for me....

Nursing homes do fulfill an important function.

Lissy F. Jarvik, quoted in *Los Angeles Times*, April 17, 1988.

A suspicion takes shape in my mind. Is this season so hard for me because when I look into the faces near me, I see myself and my future? Can it be that, after all, my deepest fears are for myself?

Why can't we all make a choice, while awareness is still with us, as to whether or not we want to live this sort of sad half-life?

January 11, 1988: I have horrible dreams almost nightly: my mother dying in agony, a grandchild disappearing, myself buried in sliding sand, unable to cry out for help from people nearby. I wake up drenched in perspiration, shaking, crying. Breakfast is little comfort. Food, with rare exceptions, is tasteless, difficult to swallow. I walk from room to room, but the view from every window is bleak and hostile. The trees are gaunt, naked caricatures of their summer selves. Close to panic, I telephone a close friend in California who is a therapist.

"Genie," I say, "Why am I so miserable? Mom is being taken care of, I have time to myself—too much, it seems. I feel paralyzed. I sit for hours and stare at the most stupid television programs. . . ."

"I'm not surprised," she says. "You're suffering from loss of purpose and feeling isolated. You miss your friends and the familiarity of your life here." She is a successful writer and knows I share her interest. After reassuring me that I'm not losing my mind, she gives me an assignment to write one page a day on any subject and send her a copy of my first week's output. "Don't worry about good writing. Just be honest. If it's nothing more than a diatribe against ice and snow, that's okay."

I hang up, feeling a little encouraged.

Companionship

February 2, 1988: My mother and Belle help fold laundry with other residents in the dining area. Staff people compliment them all on the job they do. It isn't bridge, but it's companionship.

Belle tells me she and Mom have been friends since they were young girls. I don't correct her.

Sometimes, I eat a meal with them, but today I leave for a dental appointment just as they are sitting down to wait for their lunch trays. I glance back as I reach the door of the dining hall. My mother has put her head down on the table on her folded arms. Weariness? Sadness? I wish I knew.

May 8, 1988: It's Mother's Day, and one of Belle's daughters and I plan to make a two-family party of it in the Activity Room. Several of Belle's seven living children are there. She is near the head of the table; Mom and I are at the other end. One of the daughters has brought fresh yeast rolls, homemade peach preserves, and real butter; the kitchen has prepared a feast of turkey and trimmings.

Belle is confused by all the visitors. Like Mom, she is rarely sure who's who. Also, her sight is not much better than her hearing. She strains to see the far end of the table. "Who's that?" she asks over and over, pointing toward my mother. "That's Emily, your roommate," Belle's daughter, Jane, tells her each time. By the time Belle asks again, we are all in high spirits, and Jane answers, "Oh, that's just another one of your kids, Mom." I am amazed when my mother answers, "Yes, I'm the youngest one!" It nearly breaks up the party. I never think of asking for a miracle, but this is one. My mother has not been intentionally humorous in years. . . .

July 21, 1988: I have come to a decision which surprises me: I think my mother is actually happier here than she was at home with me. There, she lay on the sofa most of the day while I sat at my word processor, my earphones making even casual conversation impossible. Now, she is never bored. There are aides in and out of the room all day. Her excursions down the hall to be lifted into and out of her bath by a hydraulic contraption are small adventures. There are exercise classes in which residents sit in a circle and move whatever still answers the command, mostly arms, of course. Various clergymen rotate Sunday services. All holidays are observed with decorations and activities. There is even one called "Harvest Day" with prizewinning vegetables displayed on bales of hay out in front and a hayride in a horse-drawn wagon for those able to manage it. With so many companions of similar age, she is free of the "last leaf on the tree" syndrome.

There is also a weekly class on Colorado history, which I attend with her one day and find fascinating. Mom pays little attention, but she smiles at me a lot and pats my hand constantly. And twice a week, a mental health professional gathers certain residents, Mom and Belle among them, in the Activity Room. I don't feel that I should ask to listen in, but I understand the purpose is to help maintain stability for those who are in greatest danger of slipping away from reality. I wait at the door today for them to come out. On the way back to the room, I say, "What do you talk about in your meeting?" "I'm not sure," she answers and leans down over the chair she is pushing to shout to Belle, "What did we talk about today?" "Oh, not much of anything," is Belle's answer. Still, I sense a feeling of importance in both of them at having been singled out for special attention.

No Longer Feeling Guilty

August 2, 1988: On my way to see her today, I feel strangely lighthearted. I have cut my visits back to every other day, talking to her several times on the telephone on alternate days. I'm living life on a level new to me, walking down country roads as the day comes to life, writing, swimming, and trying to capture on film sky and clouds seen through an old barbed wire fence. Best of all, I'm no longer feeling guilty. What I considered a "last resort," I now regard as the best decision I could have made. I don't mean that it's nirvana, but both of us are several steps closer than we were before.

When I walk into the room today, she is glad to see me. She asks me several times if it's Sunday. I say, "No, Mom, it's Tuesday." She rolls Belle's wheelchair up close to where I am sitting. I read letters from relatives to her, and she seems to listen attentively. I am not prepared for her comment out of the blue while I am putting the letters back into their envelopes. "I like my life," she says. I sit, stunned, wondering if mental telepathy is operating between us. I start to tell her how happy her words make me, but the moment is gone. She pats my hand and asks again, "You say this is Sunday?"

"No data has emerged to counteract my
impression of nursing homes as death sentences."

Nursing Homes
Are Harmful

Betty Friedan

Betty Friedan is the founder of the National Organization of
Women and the author of *The Feminine Mystique*. In the following viewpoint, excerpted from her book *The Fountain of Age*,
Friedan cites research and her own experiences to illustrate the
dismal conditions—filth, neglect, and improper treatment—that
senior citizens endure in nursing homes. Friedan asserts that, almost universally, the health of the elderly deteriorates rapidly
when they enter a nursing home.

As you read, consider the following questions:

1. According to Friedan, what is the most likely cause of death?
2. How have physical restraints harmed nursing home patients,
   according to the author?
3. What is the importance of communities to the elderly, in
   Friedan's opinion?

I admit my own overwhelming dread and prejudice against nursing homes. In ten years of research, no data has emerged to counteract my impression of nursing homes as death sentences, the final interment from which there is no exit but death. In some research I have seen, no matter their condition upon entering, men or women tended to die within six months of being put in a nursing home. Even if they were not dying, or in any state of terminal disease when they entered—merely no longer able to take care of themselves, living alone, like my mother— something happened, as a result of being put in the nursing home, that led to death. Of "no apparent cause," as they said of my mother. She died in her sleep "of old age"; she was ninety. I think she had no wish to live any longer, in that nursing home; no bonds, no people she cared about, no purpose to her days.

A National Obsession

When I started out in this search, over ten years ago now, I was appalled by the overwhelming preoccupation of gerontologists with nursing homes and their sick, passive, childlike, and ever more deteriorating senile patients, when only 5 percent of people over sixty-five were, in fact, in nursing homes. Since then, the preoccupation with nursing homes as the only answer to "long-term care" for older people has become a national obsession—preventing government, national, state, and local organizations, and older people themselves, from taking real, small steps that would ensure other possible choices.

The nursing home specter had become a self-fulfilling prophecy by 1990. The number of nursing home residents had almost tripled in twenty years. Total annual expenditures on nursing home care had risen from $4.2 billion to $34.7 billion. The probability of nursing home use had increased to 17 percent for ages 65 to 74, 36 percent for ages 75 to 84, and 60 percent for ages 85 to 94. The average age of nursing home residents was now 79.

It was estimated that 37 percent of those who died at 65 years or older in 1986 were in nursing homes. Some 25 percent died within a month of entering the nursing home, 50.8 percent within six months.

An estimate in the *New England Journal of Medicine* based on National Center for Health Statistics data projected that one in seven men and one in three women who reached the age of 65 in 1990 would spend at least one year in a nursing home. "For persons who turned 65 in 1990, we project that 43% will enter a nursing home at some time before they die . . . 55% [for] at least one year . . . 21% [for] five years or more."

Pointing out that nursing home patients tend to get worse after their admission to nursing homes—they develop urinary tract infections, eye and ear infections, and bed sores—Bruce Vladeck concluded in a 1980 study, "These are diseases not of age or frailty but of inadequate care." He reported that doctors and even trained nurses were "largely absent from nursing homes" and that the ongoing care of chronically ill nursing home residents was "deficient." "They sit in these nursing homes, minds clouded by drugs, staring unfocussingly at daytime television and soon but not soon enough they are dead."

Some 5 to 10 percent die simply from being moved from home or hospital to nursing home, he stated. "Many nursing home residents would be better off anywhere else."

"The single greatest fear we have in this country is the fear of growing old, losing our mind, and being put away in a nursing home," my friend and mentor Robert Butler has been saying for years now. And women are more likely to enter nursing homes, unnecessarily, than men, according to the experts, because they are both less likely to have a spouse still alive to share their care and less willing to be a "burden" to their children; they do not want to give up their independence to be cared for by daughters or daughters-in-law.

Medicare and Medicaid

Yet, despite the focus on "catastrophic illness," most people now die as the end result of chronic conditions they've lived with a long time. Medicare does not cover long-term care, except for acute illness, nor preventive medicine or almost any home care. Only people below the poverty level are eligible for Medicaid, which covers nursing home care as well as eyeglasses, hearing aids, dental and drug prescriptions. By 1983, there were some 50 percent more people in nursing homes than in community hospitals, many with waiting lists of a year or more. But despite repeated evidence that most older people would prefer to stay in their own homes, less than 3 percent of federal Medicare funds devoted to long-term care in 1990 was spent on home services. And those nursing homes now cost over $30,000 a year. "Spending down" to poverty has become accepted as the way to get Medicaid to pay the nursing home bills. Reports in the media of what goes on in nursing homes increase our helpless obsession and denial: "When you enter a nursing home there's a feeling that this is the end. . . . You give up your home, your possessions, your autonomy. . . . Most people leave nursing homes horizontally," according to the *New York Times*.

> Relatives often go to extraordinary lengths before they send a loved one to an institution. Social workers say they know of too many daughters working themselves to exhaustion trying to attend to an infirm parent while raising families of their own, and too many husbands and wives, frail themselves, struggling for years to provide gruelling 24-hour aid to a chronically ill spouse.

The solution that the "care" experts now offer people is to "plan" and save to buy insurance to cover nursing home care, rather than question the entire specter. The *Times* continued:

> One reason nursing home costs come as such a shock to so many people is simply that they have not planned for them. . . . Americans have not traditionally thought of saving or buying insurance to cover the expenses of long-term care. . . .

> More and more, experts say, planning ahead for the possible expense of chronic care will have to be a customary rite of aging.

Nursing Home Horrors

Thus, we are advised to buy "long-term care" insurance we may not need, or that will profit a nursing home that could make us long for death. During my winter in California in 1992, the *Los Angeles Times* reported state "citations" of a "skilled nursing home" at Rancho Los Amigos for "violating new Federal regulations that restrict the drugging and physical restraint of patients and for providing so little supervision that some patients were found wandering along a highway."

> Inspectors described the facility as reeking from a "musty, fetid" odor. Floors were debris-strewn and sticky from spills and messes. A drainage bag of body fluids was found on the floor of one room. Feeding pumps and suction canisters were encrusted with secretions. In another room, a restraining device used to tie down patients was covered with ants.

> Stinking bedridden patients in dirty hospital gowns were routinely left unbathed. . . . Inspectors charged that nursing home staff failed to rotate patients every two hours to prevent development of painful bedsores and that they helped patients out of bed and into wheelchairs only every other day.

> Inspectors observed one patient whose fingernails had grown so long he could not push a button to operate a mechanical device and another patient who was left in bed for four days, clothed only in a diaper.

> According to state health inspectors the Rancho nursing home has flagrantly disregarded new Federal nursing home regulations [that] require nursing home staff to stimulate patients to attain the highest practicable physical, mental and psychosocial well-being.

> Inspectors also faulted the nursing home staff for failing to adhere to new regulations that strictly govern the use of psychoactive drugs and physical restraints. . . . They witnessed one patient who was strapped so that the restraints tightened around his genitals. In another case, a patient given psychoactive drugs suffered permanent neurological damage as a result of the medication.

. . . In the course of my search, I was plied with shocking statistics about the excessive use of physical restraints in nursing homes, denying patients any activity at all, any purpose. As to the prevalence of use of tranquilizers and anti-psychotics as restraints and their deleterious side effects, in the San Francisco Bay Area physicians' orders for such drugs in nursing homes rose by 10 percent in 1987, though the nursing home population rose by only 1 percent in that time—with documented evidence that the risk of falling increased among older people placed on such drugs.

'Why, your fever's way down!'

Reprinted by permission of *The Spectator*.

In a 1992 hearing on "the shocking problem of excessive and unjustified medication of elderly Americans living in board-and-care homes," Chairman Edward R. Roybal of the House Select Committee on Aging reported on a three-year investigation of nursing homes in Ohio, Texas, California, and Washington, D.C.:

> Residents of these facilities were excessively medicated—over 85 percent of them were on three prescribed drugs a day, two of which were psychoactive, despite the fact that not one home maintained medical or mental health records to justify the residents' drug use. This form of legalized drug abuse often leaves the frail residents of these homes in a stuporous condition.

Lloyd Lewis, executive director of two continuing-care facilities, Kendal at Longwood and Crosslands in Pennsylvania, who boasted that "in 17 years of operating our nursing centers we have never owned or used physical restraints," wanted to mount a nationwide effort to "untie the elderly" as a major confrontation of ageism in America. He showed me data that restraints (belts, vests, jackets) supposedly intended to "protect" the elderly, but sometimes suffocating or strangling them, are used on more than a third of the nursing home population, at least a half million Americans every day. The *Minnesota Star Tribune* (December 2, 1990), in an eight-month investigation of deaths caused by use of restraints in Minnesota nursing homes, found "cases of people strangling in their chairs, dangling from their beds, hanging or falling or burning to death." This was sixteen years after a congressional committee heard "complaint after complaint about old people tied up like animals in nursing homes" and adopted rules to prohibit use of such restraints "for staff convenience," requiring doctors' orders that they were "needed to prevent injury."

Jury-Awarded Damages

A few nursing homes have been made to pay multi-million-dollar damages for deaths caused by "isolated acts of gross negligence." However, for the first time, a federal jury in Mississippi in 1990 awarded damages to families of two nursing home patients "whose last years were blighted by neglect at a home run by the nation's largest nursing home chain . . . the kind of routine neglect and abuse that do not kill but cause great suffering for thousands of nursing home patients every day."

The cases involved Beverly Enterprises, then operating more than eight hundred nursing homes around the country. The Jackson, Mississippi, jury awarded damages to the families of Margie Berryhill and Frederick Bolion for "what happens to residents in maybe 60 percent of the nation's nursing homes," as one expert put it. The jury assigned dollar amounts to the different kinds of neglect, according to *New York Times* writer Tamara Lewin:

> Fifty thousand dollars for leaving Mrs. Berryhill in her own excrement, $25,000 for verbal abuse of her by the staff, $15,000 for not bathing Mr. Bolion, $15,000 for keeping him in a smelly room, $60,000 for failing to give him the physical therapy he needed, and so on, coming to a total of $125,000 for each of them. The jury further found that Beverly Enterprises' failure to provide good care was so "willful, wanton, malicious or callous" as to merit another $125,000 in punitive damages to each claimant.

Ironically, the verdict in one of these cases was reversed because the evidence in the other was so "inflammatory and shocking" that it had unduly influenced the verdict in the other.

Ultimately, however, both cases were settled.

But nursing home "reform" may not be the answer. Even some of the best nursing homes, in fact, the very premises upon which nursing homes in America are run, *deny the personhood of age*. They merely represent an extreme case of ageism, reifying the image of age as inevitable decline and deterioration. We are right to dread the nursing home. If we are not seen as human beings, but merely "objects" to be disposed of, warehoused until death, then restraints, drugs, are not "abuse" but cost-efficient aids to our "long-term care.". . .

Wanting to Stay Home

It has become very clear that old people want to stay in their own homes, where they have bonds and projects, and can control their own lives, whatever disabilities they may have, which often don't involve serious declines in function until they are well into their eighties. Even in their eighties, when a sizable percentage of the elderly may have some disability, they continue to *function*, as long as they stay in their own community. Elizabeth Bartoch, eighty-three, of Cresskill, New Jersey, had amnesia after her husband died in her arms. She was "distressed" at her confusion. Her son closed up her tiny house, she said goodbye to her neighbors, and moved in with his family fifteen miles away. But after fourteen months, she decided she wanted to go home again. Her son said: "She felt she was intruding. She wanted to do things her way, but it wasn't her home." Back in her own home, she took in a boarder, and her son stopped by every day. "She's happy to be back in her familiar neighborhood where she can take walks without getting lost."

Over these years, I have visited some of the very best nursing homes, sparkling clean, where neither physical nor chemical restraints were used, and the halls and rooms certainly did not smell of urine and feces or that awful, all-pervading sweet smell of disinfectant. Run by Jewish and Catholic agencies, not-for-profit, some were doing their best to give the residents some "choice"—over the food they ate, which movie to see—and some control of their day, at least the illusion of some choice over when they wake or sleep or eat. But basically the institutional paradigm remained: They left the larger community of which they were part, and their identity in it, when they entered the nursing home. Within the institution, how much control could they have over their own lives, how much real choice?

3

VIEWPOINT

"In the struggle between young and old for resources, the young should be given the advantage."

Health Care for the Elderly Should Be Limited

Daniel Callahan

Daniel Callahan is the director of the Hastings Center, a research organization in Briarcliff Manor, New York, devoted to ethical issues in medicine. In the following viewpoint, Callahan argues that because the elderly have lived longer than younger people and because of high medical costs, health care for the elderly should be limited so that society can meet the needs of the young. Callahan contends that there is no obligation to help the elderly live as long as they desire. Callahan is the author of *Setting Limits: Medical Goals in an Aging Society* and *What Kind of Life: The Limits of Medical Progress*.

As you read, consider the following questions:

1. How much more does government spend on health care for the elderly than for the young, according to Callahan?
2. In the author's opinion, what social needs should not be jeopardized by addressing health care for the elderly?
3. According to Callahan, who should take the lead in recognizing the importance of younger generations?

One of the most important moral principles in any society is that of the reciprocal obligations of young and old. The old are bound to care for the dependent young, and the young, when able, to care for the dependent old. When life expectancies were short, medicine primitive and ineffective, and illness brief, there was no special problem with this principle. Each age group could do its duty. This once common situation has given way to a different situation: health care for the elderly threatens to destroy the earlier symmetry, placing new and unprecedented demands on the young.

Why is this happening? The answer is not necessarily found in a change of the ratio of young to old (although that is a factor), or in the costs for an aging population as such (also a factor), but in an intensification of expensive technological treatments for the elderly. The combination of a growing number and proportion of the elderly and the application of constant medical progress to them is the main engine of rising costs for the elderly. The fastest growing group of those on kidney dialysis, for instance, are over age seventy. Also, complex surgical procedures are now performed on the elderly in a way that would have been unthinkable even a decade ago.

A Great Discrepancy

As a consequence of these developments, some 30 percent of the federal health budget now goes to the elderly (with a predicted increase to 50 percent in the next ten to twenty years). Seven to eight times more government money is spent on health care for the old than for the young. The contrast, say, between what we pay a primary school teacher to teach the young and what we pay a physician to take care of the old is striking.

These are unpleasant facts. Great leaps of hope and faith have been made to tame them. It is said, for instance, that since we will all age, everyone will eventually benefit from present policies. This may be true, provided the young are able to make it to old age in a society as affluent as the one in which their parents grew up. In our present society the young are, in fact, losing many opportunities of growing old in the best possible fashion; and the country can hardly afford poorly educated or socially maladjusted young people. It has also been said that, if we simply had a more efficient health care system and assessed the efficacy of the care provided for the elderly more carefully, we could hold down the costs to a more tolerable level.

However, we have not learned to hold down costs, and the experience of European countries is now beginning to suggest that, even with a far more cost-effective health care system, the problem of the elderly is still enormous and daunting. Or it has been claimed that more research money will lead to a cure of those ailments of old age, which are driving up health care costs. Even if this is true, such an approach generally increases rather than reduces costs. Usually it is more expensive than inexpensive ways of sustaining life that are found. This is hardly surprising in the face of the chronic and degenerative diseases of aging people. It is a fallacy, however understandable, to extrapolate from past medical success with infectious diseases to equal success with the diseases of aging. Simple immunization against Alzheimer's disease, or cancer, might someday be possible—but it is not probable. In the former case, the struggle was with exogenous pathological forces; with the latter, the struggle is with the endogenous biology of aging.

Possibilities and Problems

If these hopeful ways out of the technological trap are not in fact likely to yield a solution, then we have a terrible situation on our hands, not easily amenable to a happy economic or political outcome. The problem may be posed this way. If we continue to believe the elderly are entitled to whatever medical progress might bring in the way of saving and extending life, then there are an infinite number of future medical possibilities and a no less infinite number of ways to spend money in pursuing them; that is, a struggle against mortality itself. If, however, we recognize that we may have to set some boundaries in that struggle, then it can easily appear as if we hold the lives of the elderly in low regard, as somehow less valuable than the lives of the young. If we choose to ignore age altogether in allocating resources—meeting legitimate medical needs only in an age-blind way—then the elderly will inevitably have greater needs; those needs will necessarily trump the needs of other age groups.

Is there an escape from these problems? Yes, but only if we are willing and able to rethink some moral and social assumptions about our obligations to the elderly. Three ingredients of a possible approach can be suggested. Neither the elderly nor any other age group can make unlimited claims on resources, nor can the old make unlimited claims on the young. I do not think anyone would really disagree with this idea, but we have been affluent enough in the past so that we never had to invoke it. Now we do. Some relative priority has to be established between the needs of the young and those of the old; a pure age-egalitarianism makes neither economic nor moral sense. I would state the priority this way: Every young person should have an opportunity to become an old person, and it is only fair to limit assistance to those already old to make that possible— the elderly already have that which the young lack.

Given a whole range of social needs—housing, education, economic development, and so on—it makes no sense to jeopardize meeting them to find and pay for endless ways of improving the health and lengthening the lives of the elderly. If we must set limits on health care for the elderly then we need to fashion a fresh view of old age, and a range of services appropriate to the needs of the elderly. Such a view should encompass a far better balance, than exists at present, between caring and social services and high-technology curative medicine. Our present system is enormously biased toward the latter, as the Medicare program makes obvious.

What I suggest would also encompass a perception easily obtainable: There is no necessary correlation between length of life and human happiness (at least once an early, premature death has been avoided). The fact that some people want to live to 100 does not mean that we are obliged to shape public policy to help them obtain that goal. A long life, yes; a very long life, no.

Rationing by Age

There are conditions under which a health-care system that rationed life-extending resources by age would be the prudent choice and therefore the choice that constituted a just or fair distribution of resources between age groups.

Norman Daniels, *Am I My Parents' Keeper?* 1988.

Probably the worst legacy of medical progress has been to transform our view of old age into a kind of medical accident. Since it is true that many diseases once associated with aging can be treated effectively, it has become common to think that there is no necessary correlation between becoming sick and getting old; medicine constantly works to separate the two categories.

At the same time, the notion is conveyed from many sources that a good old age is one that preserves the physical and mental vitality of middle age; if age takes its toll it is only because we have yet to learn how to control the illnesses and infirmities that seem to go with it. They can all be eradicated given enough ingenuity and money for science.

An important result of this kind of thinking, combined with a cultural proclivity for glorifying youth, has been to rob old age of meaning and significance. How can it have those values if it is nothing more than a reflection of the present state of the medical arts, not something intrinsic to the condition itself.

Perhaps the deepest question that must be faced here is this: How should we allocate our resources between the present and the future? The elderly are with us, here and now. They have serious health needs and they most likely will always have such needs regardless of future medical advances. Yet, it is also true, however unappealing to say so, that the future lies always with the young rather than the old. The primary duty of a society is to make certain that it has a future, and that those who will inherit that future are well prepared to do so. In the struggle between young and old for resources, the young should be given the advantage. If they are not, then there will be no decent future for them or for the elderly people they will become.

The elderly themselves should be the first to understand this. Their own youth, and much of their welfare, rested upon the work and contributions of earlier generations, upon those who were once their elders. The young should not be put in the position of forcing the elderly to make sacrifices or to give way to the young. The elderly should lead the way. They should be the first to say that the needs of the young must take precedence over their own needs. This is being both gracious and fair.

*"Most doctors and a majority of the public . . .
oppose terminating care to people who are
conscious, even if there is little prospect for
recovery."*

Health Care for
the Elderly Should
Not Be Limited

Amitai Etzioni

Amitai Etzioni is a professor at George Washington University
in Washington, D.C., and is the editor of the *Responsive Community*, a quarterly communitarian journal. In the following viewpoint, Etzioni argues that Daniel Callahan's proposal to ration
health care to elderly persons based on their age is wrong because the elderly are living longer, healthier, and more productive lives. Etzioni contends that health care rationing based on
one's age raises the possibility of further rationing applied to
other "so-called unproductive" segments of the population.

As you read, consider the following questions:

1. What does Etzioni mean when he says that Callahan wants
   the elderly to trade "quantity for quality"?
2. According to Etzioni, what technologies would Callahan
   withhold from elderly patients?
3. What are two of the factors that would work against health
   care rationing for the elderly, in the author's opinion?

Amitai Etzioni, "Spare the Old, Save the Young," *Nation*, June 11, 1988. Reprinted with
permission from the *Nation* magazine; © The Nation Company, L.P.

In the coming years, Daniel Callahan's call to ration health care for the elderly, put forth in his book *Setting Limits*, is likely to have a growing appeal. Practically all economic observers expect the United States to go through a difficult time as it attempts to work its way out of its domestic (budgetary) and international (trade) deficits. Practically every serious analyst realizes that such an endeavor will initially entail slower growth, if not an outright cut in our standard of living, in order to release resources to these priorities. When the national economic "pie" grows more slowly, let alone contracts, the fight over how to divide it up intensifies. The elderly make an especially inviting target because they have been taking a growing slice of the resources (at least those dedicated to health care) and are expected to take even more in the future. Old people are widely held to be "nonproductive" and to constitute a growing "burden" on an ever-smaller proportion of society that is young and working. Also, the elderly are viewed as politically well organized and powerful; hence "their" programs, especially Social Security and Medicare, have largely escaped . . . attempts to scale back social expenditures, while those aimed at other groups—especially the young, but even more so future generations—have been generally curtailed. There are now some signs that a backlash may be forming.

Generation War

If a war between the generations, like that between the races and between the genders, does break out, historians may accord former Governor Richard Lamm of Colorado the dubious honor of having fired the opening shot in his statement that the elderly ill have "got a duty to die and get out of the way." Phillip Longman, in his book *Born to Pay*, sounded an early alarm. However, the historians may well say, it was left to Daniel Callahan, a social philosopher and ethicist, to provide a detailed rationale and blueprint for limiting the care to the elderly, explicitly in order to free resources for the young. Callahan's thesis deserves close examination because he attempts to deal with the numerous objections his approach raises. If his thesis does not hold, the champions of limiting funds available to the old may have a long wait before they will find a new set of arguments on their behalf.

In order to free up economic resources for the young, Callahan offers the older generation a deal: Trade quantity for quality; the elderly should not be given life-*extending* services but better years while alive. Instead of the relentless attempt to push death to an older age, Callahan would stop all development of life-extending technologies and prohibit the use of ones at hand for those who outlive their "natural" life span, say, the age of 75. At the same time, the old would be granted more palliative medicine (e.g., pain killers) and more nursing-home and home-health care, to make their natural years more comfortable.

Callahan's call to break an existing ethical taboo and replace it with another raises the problem known among ethicists and sociologists as the "slippery slope." Once the precept that one should do "all one can" to avert death is given up, and attempts are made to fix a specific age for a full life, why stop there? If, for instance, the American economy experiences hard times in the 1990s, should the "maximum" age be reduced to 72, 65—or lower? And should the care for other so-called unproductive groups be cut off, even if they are even younger? Should countries that are economically worse off than the United States set their limit, say, at 55?

Redefining the Concept of Death

This is not an idle thought, because the idea of limiting the care the elderly receive in itself represents a partial slide down such a slope. Originally, Callahan, the Hastings Center (which he directs) and other think tanks played an important role in redefining the concept of death. Death used to be seen by the public at large as occurring when the lungs stopped functioning and, above all, the heart stopped beating. In numerous old movies and novels, those attending the dying would hold a mirror to their faces to see if it fogged over, or put an ear to their chests to see if the heart had stopped. However, high technology made these criteria obsolete by mechanically ventilating people and keeping their hearts pumping. Hastings et al. led the way to provide a new technological definition of death: brain death. Increasingly this has been accepted, both in the medical community and by the public at large, as the point of demise, the point at which care should stop even if it means turning off life-extending machines, because people who are brain dead do not regain consciousness. At the same time, most doctors and a majority of the public as well continue strongly to oppose terminating care to people who are conscious, even if there is little prospect for recovery, despite considerable debate about certain special cases.

Callahan now suggests turning off life-extending technology for all those above a certain age, even if they could recover their full human capacity if treated. It is instructive to look at the list of technologies he would withhold: mechanical ventilation, artificial resuscitation, antibiotics and artificial nutrition and hydration. Note that while several of these are used to maintain brain-dead bodies, they are also used for individuals who are temporarily incapacitated but able to recover fully; indeed, they are used to save young lives, say, after a car accident. But there is no way to stop the development of such new technologies and the improvement of existing ones without depriving the young of benefit as well. (Antibiotics are on the list because of an imminent "high cost" technological advance—administering them with a pump implanted in the body, which makes their introduction more reliable and better distributes dosages.)

The Medical Establishment

Once such an arbitrary variable as age is allowed to be used by the government and the medical establishment to decide who shall receive "aggressive" medical care—then the door is open for such criteria as race, religion and social class to be similarly used.

Michael Klausner, *Wall Street Journal*, February 24, 1988.

One may say that this is Callahan's particular list; other lists may well be drawn. But any of them would start us down the slope, because the savings that are achieved by turning off the machines that keep brain-dead people alive are minimal compared with those that would result from the measures sought by the people calling for new equity between the generations. And any significant foray into deliberately withholding medical care for those who can recover does raise the question, Once society has embarked on such a slope, where will it stop?

Age Limits

Those opposed to Callahan, Lamm and the other advocates of limiting care to the old, but who also favor extending the frontier of life, must answer the question, Where will the resources come from? One answer is found in the realization that defining people as old at the age of 65 is obsolescent. That age limit was set generations ago, before changes in life styles and medicines much extended not only life but also the number and quality of productive years. One might recognize that many of the "elderly" can contribute to society not merely by providing love, companionship and wisdom to the young but also by continuing to work, in the traditional sense of the term. Indeed, many already work in the underground economy because of the large penalty—a cut in Social Security benefits—exacted from them if they hold a job "on the books."

Allowing elderly people to retain their Social Security benefits while working, typically part-time, would immediately raise significant tax revenues, dramatically change the much-feared dependency-to-dependent ratio, provide a much-needed source of child-care workers and increase contributions to Social Security (under the assumption that anybody who will continue to work will continue to contribute to the program). There is also evidence that people who continue to have meaningful work will live longer and healthier lives, without requiring more health care, because psychic well-being in our society is so deeply associated with meaningful work. Other policy changes, such as deferring retirement, modifying Social Security benefits by a small, gradual stretching out of the age of full-benefit entitlement, plus some other shifts under way, could be used readily to gain more resources. Such changes might be justified prima facie because as we extend life and its quality, the payouts to the old may also be stretched out.

Beyond the question of whether to cut care or stretch out Social Security payouts, policies that seek to promote intergenerational equity must be assessed as to how they deal with another matter of equity: that between the poor and the rich. A policy that would stop Federal support for certain kinds of care, as Callahan and others propose, would halt treatment for the aged, poor, the near-poor and even the less-well-off segment of the middle class (although for the latter at a later point), while the rich would continue to buy all the care they wished to. Callahan's suggestion that a consensus of doctors would stop certain kinds of care for all elderly people is quite impractical; for it to work, most if not all doctors would have to agree to participate. Even if this somehow happened, the rich would buy their services overseas either by going there or by importing the services. There is little enough we can do to significantly enhance economic equality. Do we want to exacerbate the inequalities that already exist by completely eliminating access to major categories of health care services for those who cannot afford to pay for them?

Slipping Down the Slope

In addition to concern about slipping down the slope of less (and less) care, the *way* the limitations are to be introduced raises a serious question. The advocates of changing the intergenerational allocation of resources favor rationing health care for the elderly but nothing else. This is a major intellectual weakness of their argument. There are other major targets to consider within health care, as well as other areas, which seem, at least by some criteria, much more inviting than terminating care to those above a certain age. Within the medical sector, for example, why not stop all interventions for which there is no hard evidence that they are beneficial? Say, public financing of psychotherapy and coronary bypass operations? Why not take the $2 billion or so from plastic surgery dedicated to face lifts, reducing behinds and the like? Or require that all burials be done by low-cost cremations rather than using high-cost coffins? . . .

159

Last but not least, as the United States enters a time of economic constraints, should we draw new lines of conflict or should we focus on matters that sustain our societal fabric? During the 1960s numerous groups gained in political consciousness and actively sought to address injustices done to them. The result has been some redress and an increase in the level of societal stress (witness the deeply troubled relationships between the genders). But these conflicts occurred in an affluent society and redressed deeply felt grievances. Are the young like blacks and women, except that they have not yet discovered their oppressors—a group whose consciousness should be raised, so it will rally and gain its due share?

The answer is in the eye of the beholder. There are no objective criteria that can be used here the way they can be used between the races or between the genders. While women and minorities have the same rights to the same jobs at the same pay as white males, the needs of the young and the aged are so different that no simple criteria of equity come to mind. Thus, no one would argue that the teen-agers and those above 75 have the same need for schooling or nursing homes.

At the same time, it is easy to see that those who try to mobilize the young—led by a Washington research group, Americans for Generational Equity (AGE), formed to fight for the needs of the younger generation—offer many arguments that do not hold. For instance, they often argue that today's young, age 35 or less, will pay for old people's Social Security, but by the time that they come of age they will not be able to collect, because Social Security will be bankrupt. However, this argument is based on extremely farfetched assumptions about the future. In effect, Social Security is now and for the foreseeable future overprovided, and its surplus is used to reduce deficits caused by other expenditures . . . in what is still an integrated budget. And, if Social Security runs into the red again somewhere after the year 2020, relatively small adjustments in premiums and payouts would restore it to financial health.

Above all, it is a dubious sociological achievement to foment conflict between the generations, because, unlike the minorities and the white majority, or men and women, many millions of Americans are neither young nor old but of intermediate ages. We should not avoid issues just because we face stressing times in an already strained society; but maybe we should declare a moratorium on raising new conflicts until more compelling arguments can be found in their favor, and more evidence that this particular line of divisiveness is called for.

Periodical Bibliography

The following articles have been selected to supplement the diverse views presented in this chapter. Addresses are provided for periodicals not indexed in the *Readers' Guide to Periodical Literature*, the *Alternative Press Index*, or the *Social Sciences Index*.

Judy Briggs — "Home Care for the Disabled Elderly," *World Health*, July/August 1994.

Consumer Reports — "Nursing Homes: When a Loved One Needs Care," August 1995.

Joseph Epstein — "License to Steal: How Nursing Homes Are Cashing In Big on Health Care Cost Containment," *Financial World*, September 26, 1995. Available from 1328 Broadway, New York, NY 10001-2116.

Esther B. Fein — "As Competition Expands, Nursing Homes Diversify," *New York Times*, April 30, 1994.

L. Freeman — "Home-Sweet-Home Health Care," *Monthly Labor Review*, March 1995.

Andrew M. Kramer — "Health Care for Elderly Persons—Myths and Realities," *New England Journal of Medicine*, April 13, 1995. Available from 10 Shattuck St., Boston, MA 02115-6094.

Penelope Lemov — "Nursing Homes and Common Sense," *Governing*, July 1994.

David Levine — "Your Aging Parents: Choosing a Nursing Home," *American Health*, June 1995.

Sue Shellenbarger — "The Aging of America Is Making 'Elder Care' a Big Workplace Issue," *Wall Street Journal*, February 16, 1994.

Amanda Spake — "Home-Care Crisis," *New Choices for Retirement Living*, March 1995.

Joseph Y. Stewart — "'My Life Is Not My Own,'" *Los Angeles Times*, May 29, 1995. Available from Reprints, Times Mirror Square, Los Angeles, CA 90012-3816.

Lois Wyse — "The Way We Are," *Good Housekeeping*, May 1995.

How Does Society View Aging and the Elderly?

Chapter Preface

While traveling from Connecticut to New York City one day, author Ram Dass (Sanskrit for "servant of God"), a former Harvard University professor, was offered the choice of a "regular" or a half-fare "senior citizen" train ticket. He recalled:

> I realized then, "I am a senior citizen." I had never put those words together. I started feeling how society defines me as old. Being a senior citizen is not necessarily a bargain. Our society is so youth-oriented it treats older people as "less than."

Pat Moore took an extreme step to experience such treatment firsthand. Disguised as a poor 85-year-old woman in New York City, the 25-year-old encountered condescension, impatience, hostility, and was even brutally mugged. According to Moore, "Young people tend to focus on what they see as the disadvantages of being older, believing that above all else, to be old is to be ugly."

Ram Dass and authors such as Betty Friedan and Gail Sheeh, have worked to combat the perception of elderly persons as incompetent or obsolete "geezers." In the words of Friedan, "We have to break through that mystique of age as only decline and deterioration, as a problem for society." Rather than as a problem, Friedan and others view the elderly as a group that can benefit younger people and society. According to California physician Katherine Dowling, "Many older persons are out there tutoring disadvantaged children, working in thrift shops, teaching nonliterate adults, and as retirees, advising young employees in their areas of expertise." To these observers, senior citizens are crucial for maintaining the strength of communities and civic life.

Negative attitudes toward the elderly may appear commonplace or dominant, but many people strive to perceive aging in positive terms. Society's disparate views toward aging and the elderly are explored in this chapter.

> *"The signs of denial and anxiety over aging permeate every aspect of our lives."*

Society Fears Aging

Jere Daniel

According to Jere Daniel, the author of the following viewpoint, a growing number of experts are part of a movement to change society's fear and denial of aging. Daniel argues that fear of aging is manifested in stereotypes about aging that develop early in childhood, endure with age, and become expectations among people growing older. Daniel contends that fear of aging may become a self-fulfilling prophecy, in which fear of physical or mental decline actually results in those conditions. Daniel is a Brooklyn, New York, freelance and radio/television writer specializing in health and human behavior.

As you read, consider the following questions:

1. What is "conscious aging," according to Stephan Rechtschaffen, cited by Daniel?
2. According to Daniel, how early in life are negative stereotypes toward aging developed?
3. In the author's opinion, who accumulates wisdom?

Jere Daniel, "Learning to Love (Gulp!) Growing Old," *Psychology Today*, September/October 1994, pp. 61–70. Reprinted with permission from *Psychology Today* magazine; ©1994 Sussex Publishers, Inc.

Technically, they are still baby boomers. But on the cusp of 50, much to their surprise, having come late into maturity, they can suddenly envision themselves becoming obsolete, just as their fathers, mothers, grandparents, uncles, and aunts did when they crossed the age-65 barrier, the moment society now defines as the borderline between maturity and old age.

Although they may be unprepared psychologically, they are certainly fortified demographically to notice the problems their elders now face—isolation, loneliness, lack of respect, and above all, virtual disenfranchisement from the society they built. The number of people reaching the increasingly mythic retirement age of 65 has zoomed from about seven and a half million in the 1930s (when Social Security legislation decreed 65 as the age of obsolescence) to 34 million today. By the turn of the century, that figure will be 61.4 million.

Changing Attitudes

If the boomers' luck holds out, they will be spared what amounts to the psychological torture of uselessness and burdensomeness that every graying generation of the twentieth century has faced before them. For there is an attitude shift in the wind. In an irony that boomers will no doubt appreciate (as rebellion is an act usually reserved for the young), a revolution in attitude about age is coming largely from a corner of the population that has traditionally been content to enjoy the status quo—a cultural elite whose median age is surely over 65.

A small but growing gaggle of experts (themselves mostly elders)—a diverse lot of gerontologists, physicians, psychologists, sociologists, anthropologists, philosophers, ethicists, cultural observers, and spiritual leaders—are the vanguard of a movement to change the way society looks at and deals with growing old. They seek to have us stop viewing old age as a problem—as an incurable disease, if you will—to be "solved" by spending billions of dollars on plastic surgery in an attempt to mask visible signs of aging, other billions on medical research to extend the life span itself, and billions more on nursing and retirement homes as a way to isolate those who fail at the quest to deny aging.

Separately and together, this cultural elite is exploring ways to move us and our social institutions toward a new concept of aging, one they call "conscious aging." They want us to be aware of and accept what aging actually is—a notice that life has not only a beginning and a middle but an end—and to eliminate the denial that now prevents us from anticipating, fruitfully using, and even appreciating what are lost to euphemism as "the golden years."

"Conscious aging is a new way of looking at and experiencing aging that moves beyond our cultural obsession with youth toward a respect and need for the wisdom of age," explains Stephan Rechtschaffen, M.D., a holistic physician who directs the Omega Institute, a kind of New Age think tank that is a driving force in this attitude shift. He would have us:

• Recognize and accept the aging process and all that goes with it as a reality, a natural part of the life cycle; it happens to us all. The goal is to change the prevailing view of aging as something to be feared and the aged as worthless.

• Reverse our societal attitude of aging as an affliction, and instead of spending billions on walling off the aging, spend more to improve the quality of life among the aged.

"I can assure you that your first gray hair is not reason enough for me to see you."

Our denial of aging has its costs. Rechtschaffen is adamant that it is not merely our elders who suffer. Quoting the late psychoanalyst Erik Erikson, he says, "Lacking a culturally viable ideal of old age, our civilization does not really harbor a concept of the whole of life."

We now live, and die, psychologically and spiritually incomplete. It may be a troubling sense of incompleteness that most stirs an appreciation for age among the baby boomers, so unfamiliar is any sense of incompleteness to the generation that invented the possibility of and has prided itself on "having it all.". . .

Curiosity About Age and Death

Until now, the conventional wisdom has been that only the aged, or those approaching its border, worry about its consequences: rejection, isolation, loneliness, and mandated obsolescence. Only they care about how they can give purpose to this final stage of their lives.

Sherwin Nuland has clear new evidence to the contrary. His book, *How We Die*, paints a shimmeringly lucid and remarkably unsentimental picture of death—the process and its meaning to the dying and to those around them. The biggest group of readers of this best-seller? Not the elderly, as most observers, and even the author himself, had anticipated. It's the baby boomers. Curiosity about age and death is booming among the boomers.

"The baby boomers, who started out rejecting the wisdom and experience of anyone over 30, are buying my book in droves," Nuland said. "To young people, death is an abstract concept. But face-to-face with aging parents and illnesses like cancer and strokes among themselves, newly graying baby boomers stare into their own mortality totally unprepared. Now this best-educated of all our generations wants information and doesn't want to turn away from what it's been trying to escape—the effects of getting old."

Fear and Denial

We fear and deny aging, the Omega experts emphasize, because we fear and deny death. "In our denial of death and the aging of the body, we have rejected the wisdom of the aged, and in doing so have robbed old age of its meaning and youth of its direction," Rechtschaffen asserts. We pretend that old age can be turned into a kind of endless middle age, thereby giving young people a false road map to the future, one that does not show them how to plan for their whole life, gain insight into themselves, or to develop spiritually.

The signs of denial and anxiety over aging permeate every aspect of our lives. We have no role models for growing old gracefully, only for postponing it. For example:

• The vast dependence on plastic surgery specifically to hide the visual signs of aging is arguably the sharpest index of our anxiety. In just two decades, from the 1960s to the 1980s, the number of rhytidectomies, wrinkle-removing face-lifts, rose from 60,000 to an estimated 2 million a year at an annual cost of $10 billion.

• The negative view of aging is disastrously reinforced by the media. Articles and advertising never show a mature model, even in displaying fashions designed for women over 50. A Newsweek cover of a sweating, gray-haired young man bears the cover line, "Oh God . . . I'm really turning 50." Nursing home ads ask: "What shall we do about Mother?" By some sleight of mind, we not only come to accept these images, we come to expect them as truths.

Negative Stereotypes

We denigrate aging, Betty Friedan [author of *The Fountain of Age*] persuasively notes, by universally equating it with second childhood, "so negatively stereotyped that getting old has become something to dread and feel threatened by." A series of studies by psychologists Ellen Langer, Ph.D., of Harvard and University of Pennsylvania President Judith Rodin, Ph.D., (then at Yale) suggests how we grow to revile our aging selves.

Influenced by the fairy tales we hear as children, and what we see on television and hear in everyday life, we develop negative stereotypes about aging by the time we are six years old, the same age we develop negative stereotypes about race and sex. These stereotypes persist as we grow up, completely unaware that we even acquired them or granted them our unconditional acceptance. With our understanding of the subject forever frozen, we grow into old age assuming the stereotypes to be true. And we live down to them.

If there is a single myth about aging that most symbolizes our dread, it is the assumption that our memory will inevitably decline in old age. In a stunning study, psychologist Langer has demonstrated that it is our own psychology—the near-universal expectation of memory loss—that actually brings that fate upon us. The lesson to be learned is an extraordinary one: Fear of aging is the single most powerful agent creating exactly what we fear.

The negative stereotypes acquired in childhood parade across the adult life span as expectations. As people age, Langer finds, low expectations lead to "decreased effort, less use of adaptive strategies, avoidance of challenging situations, and failure to seek medical attention for disease-related symptoms."

Measuring Memory

In [a subsequent] study, Langer and Harvard colleague Rebecca Levy, Ph.D., confirm the effect of these negative stereotypes on aging Americans. Using standard psychological measurements of memory, the researchers studied two populations of people who hold their elders in high esteem—elderly mainland Chinese and older, deaf Americans—and compared them to a group of elderly mainstream Americans. In addition, the researchers compared memory retention in the elderly with younger people in all three groups.

Not only did the mainland Chinese and American deaf far outperform the mainstream Americans on four psychological memory tests, but the oldest in these two groups, especially the Chinese, performed almost as well as the youngest. Their performance was so strong even the researchers were surprised. They conclude that the results can be explained entirely by the fact that the Chinese have the most positive, active, and "internal" image of aging across the three cultures studied.

What is particularly striking about the Langer-Levy study is that it meticulously tracks how our fears, which are so culturally constructed, become self-fulfilling prophecies. "The social, psychological component of memory retention may be even stronger than we believed."

Just as our fear of memory loss can create actual memory decline, the dread of aging may be taking its toll on many other body systems.

The current collective view of aging is so relentlessly negative that neither our social institutions nor the aging themselves believe what worldwide research points to—that those of us alive today may be aging better than our parents.

Decline Is Not Inevitable

A landmark, 15-year longitudinal study of older people, begun in 1970 by Alvar Svanborg in the industrial city of Gothenburg, Sweden, showed no measurable decline in many body functions until after age 70, and very little decline by 81. Cognitive abilities were intact to at least age 75, and still intact in almost all who had reached 81, although speed at rote memory declined. "The vitality of old people in Sweden today, among the longest-lived people in the world, seems to be greater than it was only five or 10 years ago," Svanborg asserts.

American studies of healthy people aging in their own communities, as opposed to those shunted off to institutions, failed to show evidence of decline in intelligence, cognitive skills, and even memory that had appeared in all previous cross-sectional studies of aging. The combined thrust of the studies of "normal aging" is inescapable. Physical and mental decline is not inevitable. Belief that it is accelerates whatever decline occurs.

Still, we continue to mythologize and denigrate aging because we devalue death itself. "We refuse even to admit that we die of old age," says Nuland, a retired Yale surgeon, whose book embodies the proposition that death is a normal stage in the life cycle. This refusal is perpetuated by the medical profession and the law. "I cannot write 'Old Age' on a death certificate even though people over 70 die because they're over 70," he says.

"An octogenarian who dies of myocardial infarction is not simply a weather-beaten senior citizen with heart disease—he is the victim of an insidious progression that involves all of him, and that progression is called aging," Nuland says. He deplores the prevailing view of aging as a disease that can be cured and the biomedical search for a fountain of youth.

"Though biomedical science has vastly increased mankind's average life expectancy (78.6 years for American women, 71.6 for men), the maximum (114 years) has not changed in verifiable recorded history. Even the home-cultured yogurt of the Caucasus cannot vanquish nature," Nuland says. "Trying to add a few more years to the human life span is meaningless and wasteful."

Aging and Isolation

The promise of an extended life span simply adds unnecessary stress to the ability to accept aging. "An extended life span without extended awareness of the possibilities of a productive old age means we aren't sure we're living longer. Maybe we're just dying longer," says Rabbi Zalman Schachter-Shalomi, founder of a pioneering Spiritual Eldering Project at Philadelphia's B'nai Or Religious Fellowship. Schachter-Shalomi is the recipient of the first annual Conscious Aging Award by the Omega Institute. In place of fear of death we'd be better off with a belief in the possibilities of life, as long as it is lived.

"If age itself is defined as a 'problem,' then those over 65 who can no longer 'pass' as young are its carriers and must be quarantined lest they contaminate, in mind or body, the rest of society," Friedan asserts. So we banish the elderly from our midst and wall them off in nursing homes. We encourage them to isolate themselves in retirement homes and communities, in San Diego condos and Miami Beach hotels.

But isolating ourselves into ageist groups only sets the stage for a class warfare that is bound to get louder and more violent. Younger generations grow to resent the older, and vice versa. And so, says Nuland, the elderly grow demanding and greedy for health and custodial care while the rest of the population bemoans the financial drain the aged make on society, all the while feeling guilty for the situation.

With the old now successfully segregated out, Americans are in no position to exploit the benefits of age—or even to recognize or acknowledge that there are any. Which brings us to the special brand of intelligence called wisdom.

Sure, we have our "elder" statesmen, but the titles are honorary, often conferred with an underlying tinge of humor. They signify reverence for past accomplishments more than real respect for the wisdom that only elders have to contribute. Wisdom remains a very special commodity, a great natural resource that is undervalued—and almost totally untapped in doing what it's meant for: guiding the young. And there's only one way to get it.

It is not easy to talk about wisdom without lapsing into platitudes and vagueness, so a team of European researchers—no surprise there—has taken on the challenge to isolate the features of wisdom in clinical detail. From their ongoing studies of the aging mind, psychologists Paul B. Baltes and Ursula M. Staudinger, both of the Max Planck Institute for Human Development in Berlin, define wisdom:

- It's an expertise that wraps information in the human context of life and relates it to generational and historical flow.

- It is factual and procedural knowledge about the world and human affairs.

- It mingles insight and judgment involving complex and uncertain matters of the human condition; there is an appreciation for and understanding of the uncertainties of life.

- It involves a fine-tuned coordination of cognition, motivation, and emotion, knowledge about the self and other people and society.

- It carries knowledge about strategies to manage the peaks and valleys of life.

- It integrates past, present, and future.

A product of cultural and knowledge-based factors, rather than biologically based mechanics of the mind, wisdom accumulates with time—but only among those who remain open to new experiences. If we must insist on outwitting the constraints of biology, then wisdom—and not the scalpel—is our thing.

Wisdom Goes Ignored

It may be that we ignore wisdom because, especially over the lifetime of the boomers, we have come to overvalue, say, rocket science. The technological advancement of modern society has bred in us an infatuation with the data we have accumulated. "We've traded information for wisdom," Rechtschaffen offers.

We have confounded the accumulation of data with its application, or even an understanding of it. Wisdom, on the other hand, always puts information back in the context of human life.

Sherwin Nuland is a man forced by the exigencies of his profession to look time squarely in the eye. Old age, he says, is a "time to become contemplative, to recognize our value to people younger than ourselves." Now in his sixties, Nuland stopped operating when "I realized I was no longer as nimble as a 45-year-old. But I expect to continue contributing my knowledge and experience as long as possible." Unfortunately, he says, "the younger generation doesn't always accept it, from me or others. They see their elders as crotchety and selfish, their maturity and wisdom of no use—outdated. Age warfare continues."

Perhaps we don't recognize the wisdom of aging because our anxiety about the future—of the world, of ourselves—has overwhelmed our respect for history. We live, Rechtschaffen says, with only a linear sense of time. We push inexorably toward the future; the past is nothing. In other eras, we lived by a more circular sense of time, which allowed for a father's, even a grandfather's, experience to guide us. There was an intuitive apprehension—wisdom, if you will—that the way to deal with the future rests in an understanding of the past. Even today, many indigenous tribal societies and Eastern cultures live by a circular sense of time.

Finding Inner Meaning

The baby boomers have made it successfully, albeit noisily, through the first two-thirds of their lives, having rejected—indeed defying—the teachings of their elders. But the prospect of making it through the next third satisfied with their accomplishments and their selves requires they find inner meaning in their lives.

To give their lives purpose, they might turn from what Nuland calls "the hurly-burly of getting and spending" to a more contemplative life. And they might pay more attention to those who have already crossed the border into old age, to value their experience; to embrace their elders is to embrace their future selves. Perhaps, most of all, they might begin to think of their own death. After all, to be fully alive includes being fully aware of dying.

So long as we lock ourselves into an obsession with the youth culture, we can only develop age rage and dehumanize ourselves, says Betty Friedan. Those who give up their denial of age, who age consciously, "grow and become aware of new capacities they develop while aging. . . . [They] become more authentically themselves."

"In America today our core attitude about older people is that they are useless people whose lives are over."

Society Does Not Respect the Elderly

Nancy J. Osgood

Society's devaluation of old age is so prevalent and ingrained that older people may feel expendable and may choose to end their lives, Nancy J. Osgood argues in the following viewpoint. Osgood asserts that ageism—prejudice against and stereotyping of the elderly—is rampant in society. As a result, she contends, older persons are scapegoated and are imbued with a sense of helplessness and powerlessness. Osgood is a professor of social gerontology at Virginia Commonwealth University in Richmond.

As you read, consider the following questions:

1. Why did Janet Adkins resort to assisted suicide, according to Osgood?
2. In the author's opinion, from whom do Americans inherit their ideas about old age?
3. According to Mary Barrington, cited by Osgood, how could older persons consider themselves a burden?

Excerpted from Nancy J. Osgood, "Assisted Suicide and Older People—A Deadly Combination: Ethical Problems in Permitting Assisted Suicide," *Issues in Law & Medicine*, vol. 10, no. 4, Spring 1995. Reprinted by permission of the author.

On June 4, 1990, fifty-four-year-old Janet Adkins ended her life lying on a cot in the back of a Volkswagen van parked in a Michigan suburb. Aided by a retired pathologist, Dr. Jack Kevorkian, Adkins was hooked up to his homemade "suicide machine." She had a needle inserted in her arm, which first started saline flowing and then, when she pressed the button on the macabre death machine, sent first a sedative and then deadly potassium chloride flowing into her veins.

An active woman with loving children and grandchildren, Adkins had flown two thousand miles from her Oregon home to Michigan to seek Kevorkian's assistance in ending her life when she was diagnosed with Alzheimer's disease. Adkins was an active member of the Hemlock Society, an organization that supports legalizing assisted suicide in America. She made a deliberate decision to end her life rather than face the mental decline associated with senile dementia. Kevorkian, a long-time proponent of physician-assisted suicide, took that opportunity to use his suicide machine as a way of making a public statement to the medical community and the larger society that suicide is acceptable and that doctors should be willing to assist those who choose to die. . . .

Older Adults—Victims of Ageism and a Burden on Society

The fact that we have created a society that is so harsh to its old that ever-increasing numbers are choosing suicide as a solution to their problems is a sad commentary on America. To argue for the right to suicide and assisted suicide for older persons is a symbol of our devaluation of old age and our own ageism and fear of aging. This position endorses the belief that the answer to the problems of old age is suicide. Moreover, it may in fact be setting up conditions that rob older people of their right to live. Older people, living in a suicide-permissive society characterized by ageism, may come to see themselves as a burden on their families or on society and feel it is incumbent on them to take their own lives. Others may be pressured into suicide by uncaring or greedy family members. Those who need expensive medical technology to live may be denied help and die. The right to die then becomes not a right at all but rather an obligation. We may create a climate in which suicide is viewed as a rational choice. In a society that devalues old age and old people, in which older adults are seen as "expendable" and as an economic burden on younger members, older people may come to feel it is their social duty to kill themselves. As in more primitive societies in earlier historical periods, the old in America may be sacrificed for the good of the society.

The position that suicide and assisted suicide should be available for older people is not new, nor is it unique to America.

Pliny the Elder considered the existence of poisonous herbs proof of a kindly providence because it allowed people to die painlessly and quickly and thus avoid the pain and sickness of old age. Zeno, the founder of Stoic philosophy, similarly advocated suicide to avoid the pain and sickness of late life; at age ninety-eight, when he fell down and pulled his toe out of joint, he hanged himself. Socrates, who drank hemlock at seventy, also cited old age as one reason for taking his own life. In primitive societies, it was conventional, and occasionally obligatory, for old people to commit suicide or to be assisted in dying if, because of infirmity, they had become a burden on their society. The ancient Scythians regarded suicide as the greatest honor when they became too old for the nomadic life. They had themselves buried alive as soon as age or sickness troubled them. . . .

Definitions of Elder Abuse

Passive Neglect: Unintentional failure to fulfill a caretaking obligation; infliction of distress without conscious or willful intent, etc.

Psychological Abuse: Infliction of mental anguish by demanding, name-calling, insulting, ignoring, humiliating, frightening, threatening, isolating, etc.

Material/Financial Abuse: Illegally or unethically exploiting by using funds, property, or other assets of an older person for personal gain, etc.

Active Neglect: Intentional failure to fulfill caregiving obligations; infliction of physical or emotional stress or injury; abandonment; denial of food, medication, personal hygiene, etc.

Physical Abuse: Infliction of physical pain or injury; physical coercion; confinement; slapping, bruising, sexually molesting, cutting, lacerating, burning, restraining, pushing, shoving, etc.

Santa Barbara County Senior Resource Directory, 1995–1996.

In America today our core attitude about older people is that they are useless people whose lives are over. In an attempt to discover what it is like to be old in America, a young industrial designer assumed the appearance and character of an eighty-five-year-old woman. In 1979 Pat Moore, author of the book *Disguised,* began a three-year journey into the world of the old in America. With the help of a makeup artist, Moore learned to apply heavy prosthetic makeup to add decades to her twenty-six-year-old face. She bought jowls, crow's feet, under-eye bags, and extra neck skin. A white wig covered her hair. To complete the look, she wore a pair of heavy orthopedic shoes, used white gloves to hide her young hands, walked with a cane, wore a pair of spectacles to hide her youthful eyes, and stained and discolored her youthful white teeth with a special crayon. As she wandered disguised through city streets all over the United States, Moore was routinely ignored, treated rudely and crudely, and nearly beaten to death. Many people totally ignored her as if she did not exist. Others assumed she was hard of hearing and shouted at her or pushed in front of her to get on a bus or to get ahead in the grocery line. She was intentionally shortchanged when buying items at the store, an easy trick because one-dollar and ten-dollar bills look and feel the same to those with dimmed vision. Worst of all, some teenagers took pleasure in bashing her.

Moore's social experiment dramatically illustrates the ageism that exists in our society. Ageism, a term coined by Robert Butler in 1968, is similar to racism and sexism. He defined ageism as "a deep and profound prejudice against the elderly and a systematic stereotyping of and discrimination against people because they are old." In other words, ageism means "not wanting to have all those old people around." It results in a deep hatred of and aversion toward people who are old simply because they are old. Like racism and sexism, ageism is a form of prejudice and discrimination against one group in the society—in this case, the old.

Individualism

The ideological changes that occurred between 1780 and 1820, when the French and American Revolutions occurred, had a profound effect on the nature of age relations and the cultural value system in America. The emphasis on freedom and equality resulted in an individual achievement orientation, which has dominated our society for the last one hundred seventy years. It places a high value on activity, personal productivity through work, materialism, success, individual achievement, independence, and self-sufficiency. Older adults, who are no longer able to produce due to physical and mental changes or to social policies that remove them from gainful employment (such as retirement), are at a distinct disadvantage in a society dominated by such a value orientation. Demographics had a major impact on how we view and treat older people today. In 1810 the median age in America began to rise, resulting in larger numbers of people over age fifty in the population. Since the mid-1800s the number of older people in the U.S. population and the average life expectancy have increased greatly. As more people live longer, intergenerational competition for jobs and economic resources increases. Perceived economic scarcity is a factor in ageism.

Our ideas about age are inherited from the classical Greeks, who viewed aging as an unmitigated misfortune and terrible tragedy. The Greeks believed "those whom the gods love die young." Youth was the only period of life of true happiness. During the heroic age, manhood was measured by the standard of physical prowess. Old age robbed the person of such prowess and the ability to fight like a valiant warrior and robbed males of sexual powers. Early Greek and Roman writings were filled with images glorifying youth and beauty and denigrating old age, which was associated with the loss of youth and beauty. *Oedipus Rex*, written in the middle of the fifth century, depicted old age as a time of decline in physical and mental functioning. The image of the strong, young man also dominated Greek art and sculpture from the fifth through seventh centuries B.C. The love of youth is evident in the statues of young men and women of the Archaic period, the Parthenon frieze, and the well-known statue of the discus thrower that accentuates the strong, young, muscular physique of an athlete at the peak of his physical powers. Except in the Hellenistic period (323–27 B.C.), Greek sculptors never portrayed older figures.

America is also a country in which youth and beauty are highly valued. The glorification of youth and development of the youth cult in America began in the nineteenth century and grew rapidly in the twentieth, and it now flourishes in our present atmosphere of narcissism. Youth is associated with vitality, activity, and freshness. To be young is to be fully alive, exciting, attractive, healthy, and vigorous. Old age, on the other hand, is associated with decline, disease, disability, and death rather than wisdom, inner peace, and other positive qualities.

Ageism in Society

Psychological factors influence ageism in our culture. The youth cult grows out of a profound fear of growing old. Through the ages, few fears have cut as deeply into the human soul as the fear of aging. Americans especially have a stark terror of growing old. Old age is associated with loss of independence, physical disease, mental decline, loss of youthful vitality and beauty, and finally death, and old people are reminders of our own mortality. Because many people have limited contact with healthy, vibrant old people and lack accurate knowledge about the aging process, their fear escalates.

Ageism is manifested through stereotypes and myths about old people and aging. In medical circles older patients are stereotyped as "crocks" or "vegetables." Other common terms for older people are *old fuddy duddy*, *little old lady*, and *dirty old man*. Old people are thought of as being fit for little else but sitting idly in a rocking chair. Older women are referred to as *old witch, old bag,* and *old biddy.* Old men are stereotyped as *old geezers, old goats,* and *old codgers.* Common stereotypes of aging view the old as out to pasture, over the hill, and all washed up.

In American culture, several mechanisms perpetuate and communicate ageist images, stereotypes, and myths: common aphorisms, literature, the media, and humor. Aphorisms about aging and older people permeate American culture. Some of the most common include: "You can't trust anyone over forty"; "You're only as old as you feel"; and "Age before beauty." These common sayings convey the idea that age is something to be denied or feared and allude to imagined losses accompanying the aging process.

The Western heritage in literature is replete with negative images of old age, beginning with medieval works. The foolish lust of older women is described in the works of Geoffrey Chaucer and Giovanni Boccaccio. The physical ugliness and disgusting behavior of the old were frequently highlighted in fairy tales such as "Hansel and Gretel" and "Snow White," where old women are portrayed as wicked witches. The emptiness of old age is a major theme in American literature. In the poem "Gerontion," T.S. Eliot provides a description of the empty misery of an old man, "a dry brain in a dry season." In his works Eliot describes old age as an empty wasteland.

In every culture humor conveys attitudes about the aged. In our own society these attitudes are expressed through jokes, cartoons, comic strips, and birthday cards. Predominant themes include the decline of physical appearance, lessening of sexual ability, decline in mental and physical abilities, loss of attractiveness, and denial of aging. The old become the brunt of many negative and cruel jokes.

The Effects of Ageism

Ageism has many negative effects on older people in America. As they come to see themselves as old, with all of the negative connotations surrounding the status of the old in American culture, many feel they are abnormal, deviant, or marginal members of the culture. As Pat Moore described the feeling in *Disguised,* they feel like an uninvited, unwelcome guest at the family reunion. To use sociologist Erving Goffman's term, they feel they have a "spoiled identity." As a result many disengage from participation in civic, social, and other groups and become isolated. Ageism contributes to a sense of helplessness and powerlessness among older adults. If they accept the negative stereotypes and myths about old people, they may come to see themselves in negative terms. They believe they can no longer effectively live life and influence people and their environment.

Ageism results in the use of older adults as scapegoats for all of the social, political, and economic problems of the day. Arguments go something like this: The reason the federal deficit is so large is that we pay too much money out in Medicare and Social Security payments to those aged sixty-five and older. The reason the health care industry is in such a mess is that sick old people are draining all the health care resources. By categorizing the old negatively, younger members of society can see the old as different, deviant, not quite as good as the young, and possibly even as less than human. Ageism makes it easier for society to ignore the old and to shirk its economic and social responsibility to older citizens. Ageism blinds us to the many problems older men and women face and keeps older people from receiving the social, economic, and spiritual services they need and deserve. It facilitates control of younger people in power over older people by rationalizing their subordination, exploitation, and devalued status. By labeling the old as different or abnormal, it is easier for other members of the society to deny older citizens access to health care and societal resources and thus retain for the young power, status, wealth, and authority.

Euthanasia and Suicide

In a book chapter entitled "Rational Suicide Among the Elderly," Derek Humphry contends that old age is "sufficient cause to give up" even without unbearable suffering. He sees suicide as a "preemptive alternative to growing old." Mary Barrington, past president of the London-based Voluntary Euthanasia Society, in her "Apologia for Suicide" argues that a disabled older individual in poor health and in need of constant care and attention may feel a burden to the younger person(s) who must provide that care. This situation may be such that the young person is in "bondage" whether willingly or unwillingly. The older person may want to "release" the young person but has no real choice but to continue to live on. There is a strong implication in her writing that the older person who is a burden to the younger people should (has an obligation to) release younger family members from the burden of caring for her by opting for suicide. Stating the same position in even stronger terms, Dr. Glanville Williams argues for the elimination of "the senile" elderly. He writes:

> A decision concerning the senile may have to be taken within the next twenty years. The number of old people are [sic] increasing by leaps and bounds. Pneumonia, 'the old man's friend,' is now checked by antibiotics. The effects of hardship, exposure, starvation and accident are now minimized. Where is this leading us? . . . What of the drooling, helpless, disoriented old man or the doubly incontinent old woman lying log-like in bed? Is it here that the real need for euthanasia exists?

. . . As the aging population continues to expand rapidly and we as a nation continue to spend more dollars on health care costs and advanced medical technology, which are disproportionately utilized by older persons, the need for budget cutting, health care rationing, and redistribution of health and other resources becomes more pressing. Older adults are viewed as an emotional and financial burden to be borne by the younger members of society. Cries for rational suicide, the right to die, and legalized assisted suicide grow louder. It seems easier to eliminate the problem of too many expensive old people to care for, or to encourage the problem to eliminate itself through sanctions encouraging suicide, rather than to face hard moral choices about our financial spending as individuals and as a society and our appropriate obligations to our older members, who have created and improved the society we now live in.

"Our national denial and denigration of age has prevented us from viewing it as a new period of human life."

Society's Negative Perception of Aging Is Erroneous

Betty Friedan, interviewed by Leila Conners

Society's perception of the elderly as sick and feeble must change, Betty Friedan argues in the following viewpoint. Friedan asserts that the "mystique of age"—the fear of old age as inevitably leading to physical decay and disease—permeates society. She maintains that the harmful effects of such thinking are particularly evident in the health care sector, where older persons are denied autonomy and control of their own bodies. The author concludes that medical treatment should not deprive the elderly of dignity and personhood. Friedan is the author of *The Fountain of Age*. Leila Conners is an associate editor for *New Perspectives Quarterly*, a magazine covering domestic and international culture and politics.

As you read, consider the following questions:

1. In Friedan's opinion, what is negative about medical treatments or cures for the elderly?
2. How are some babies and elders a burden on the health care system, in the author's opinion?
3. According to Friedan, why should all hospitals and health plans have medical ethics committees?

Betty Friedan, interviewed by Leila Conners, "Aging and Death in the Youth Culture," *New Perspectives Quarterly*, Winter 1994, pp. 31–35. Reprinted by permission of Blackwell Publishers.

Conners: What does it mean to grow old in America? Why does America shun age?

Friedan: The mystique of age—the utter dread of programmed deterioration from youth to decay, decline and pathology, defining age only as personal disease and problem for society—is most extreme in America. Our national denial and denigration of age has prevented us from viewing it as a new period of human life. Instead, growing old is an unspeakable, unthinkable fate. Our horror of age stems from our obsession with youth; the cult of youth is the strongest here.

America is a nation of immigrants, of the young and hearty that left the old country and went West in the wagon trains. And for the children of immigrants, what could their grandparents teach them? Then came the baby boom population explosion after World War II just as the mass media began to exert its profound influence. A generation took shape that didn't trust anyone over 30, viewed 40 as traumatic, and 50 unthinkable.

No Positive Images

The image of age in America is a terrifying blank. Except for a few rich, powerful men in ads and newsmagazines, we cannot look on the face of age. Even ads selling women anti-age cream and youth dew use models in their 20s. In studies of magazines, television and movies, I found virtually no image of anyone over 65 doing anything any American would like to do.

Newspapers and newsmagazines across the country only discuss the "problem with age," the growing hordes of people refusing to die after 60, 70 or even 80, senile unproductive older men and women seen only as a burden on society and the young. Even at gerontology conferences, the focus is on senility and nursing homes; while way down in the basement is a single rogue, underground workshop on creativity in the later years.

Given this absolute lack of any positive image of age, no wonder we all deny our age and say "I may be 65, but inside I am only 17." But that doesn't work. After the fifth face lift, we don't look young, we look like mummies—inhuman. Denial results in increasing rage, rage at ourselves because we are not young. And this rage prevents us from recognizing the real possibilities of this new period of human life.

At the turn of the century life expectancy of women was 46, now it is nearly 80; for men it was 45, now it is over 72. With that new third of human life, we have to be pioneers of a new kind of age. There is a difference between those who continue to grow and develop—vital aging—and those who deteriorate and decline. It doesn't have to be a rare Grandma Moses and Pablo Picasso; I found people all across this country who do continue to grow and who no longer seek the fountain of youth

and are finding the fountain of age. Even women and men re-
covering from stroke, or living with arthritis or heart bypass can
achieve this mode of vital aging. From all the research and my
interviews the key to vital age seems to be purposes and projects and bonds of intimacy which require that older people remain a part of the larger, living, changing community.

Redefining Age

How would you, then, redefine age?

The personhood of age is an unmapped road of new possibilities. If people can resist the mystique of deterioration—which
can be self-fulfilling—people may be able to escape the adult
playpen and the communities of old people walled off in the
middle of the desert, kept far out of sight. If we can outgrow the
obsession with youth, men and women can move into age and
become more whole, more themselves. They become more
comfortable with their mistakes. They have had their troubles,
pain, tragedies and triumphs. They accept themselves as they
are and they find themselves released from belaboring the trau-
mas of their childhood, the sorrows of their youth and the inhi-
bitions and fears of their adolescence. And now they can be lib-
erated from the things that drove them in their middle years.
People no longer have to be superwoman and superman. There
can be a sense of new possibilities and adventure. We also become truth-tellers, which is not always comfortable for those
around us.

Negative Stereotypes

We tend to think in stereotypes when dealing with the aged, just
as some still conjure up prejudices about women or racial minorities. Old people are thought to be slow, intellectually impaired,
ill-tempered, complaining, childlike. These stereotypes give people an excuse to patronize us.

Bernice Balfour, *Los Angeles Times*, December 13, 1995.

---

*Most other societies look to their elders for guidance; Americans
don't often do that.*

Americans are not accustomed to the word "wisdom" because
the denial of age has been so extreme in America. But we are
ready for a paradigm shift in consciousness that takes into account an 80-year lifespan. We don't have to continue to be structured in terms of a lifespan of the past; there can be a whole different patterning and structure of work. Today, women and men
of their late 20s to 40s have enormous career pressures, working

60- to 80-hour weeks through their childbearing years; and yet we have a rigid timeclock that pushes people over 65 out of the workplace when they still have an enormous amount to give. Studies show that young people would rather have more flexibility and more autonomy in their worklives than a wage increase or benefits. A shorter workweek and options of jobsharing and flextime as an alternative to downsizing would meet the needs of women and men in their childbearing years and also enable new uses of the experience and wisdom of those over 65 in the workplace. Companies smart enough to adjust will reap bonanzas of enormous talent at their disposal.

Health Care Issues

In your book, The Fountain of Age, *you dispel the myth that old age is an illness; that, instead, age is a new phase of human life. Yet in old age, issues of health care and cure are more pronounced.*

The mystique of age, of old people being inevitably sick, senile and terminal, is not true. It is surprising to discover that only 5 percent of people over 65 have Alzheimer's, only 5 percent are senile, only 5 percent are in nursing homes at any one time and less than 10 percent will ever be. We need a paradigm shift in health care implied by the premises that age itself is not disease; that the older person, body and soul, becomes more and more her/himself, authentic and whole, unique and integrated, and can't be treated either in terms of youth or of separate mechanical parts. In terms of health care, autonomy and control of one's body, one's life is biologically as well as metaphysically the key to the fountain of age.

Our aim as a society should be to maximize human function and good human life. We do not need more expensive and costly nursing homes, exotic, high-tech machinery and overdiagnosis of disease, but more measures not necessarily medical that will enable people to continue to live independently, controlling their own lives in the community. We need to reject dehumanizing treatment that makes life no longer worth living even if we are kept technically alive. I do not underestimate important technological advances in medical care; they should be available. But we should resist the futile pursuit of new, esoteric, and pharmaceutical cures for exotic diseases and terminal illnesses—or disabilities that can be lived with but can't be cured, or where the cure is more disabling than the condition.

What is needed is a new version of the old-fashioned family doctor trained to treat the whole person because the person is more whole in age than in any other time. The diagnosis of narrow symptoms and "cure" often results in the overuse and dangerous mixing of drugs in age. Reaction to such drugs is one of the main causes of hospital admissions of older people. The medical profession, from nurse practitioners to doctors or new kind of peer counsellors, should go beyond diagnosis of specific disease to maintaining and enhancing function—that must be the focus of care for older people. If treatment of disease results in the loss of function or independence, institutionalization is the costly, undesirable result.

What do you believe should be the focus of health care reform?

Any reform of our health care system should not tamper with Social Security or Medicare. There is no fountain of age without survival and Social Security is absolutely essential. There are a great many people in America to whom Social Security makes the difference between having choice and options with age and no choice at all. For people living entirely on Social Security, it is barely enough. Even for people that have managed to save or take odd jobs, Social Security makes the difference that they be able to live a vital life.

More urgently, I am worried about intergenerational warfare that would make older people the scapegoats of the health care crisis. The suggestion now being heard that primary health resources should not be used by "greedy geezers," that it is their duty to "step aside and die," is outrageous. When people hit 60 or 65, they may have 20 or more years of healthy, vital life open to them; it should be unthinkable that we should solve the health care crisis by using triage against older people. In a country as wealthy as ours, there should be health care for everybody who needs it.

I am often reminded by people I know who have lived through the Holocaust in Austria and Germany that even before the use of the Jew as scapegoat, the idea was to exterminate "unproductive" people—the retarded, the physically handicapped and older people. That was genocide. And this concept was raised in Austria and in Germany during a period of economic crisis. Today with the rationing of health care, I worry the state might try to put limits on treatment for older people. I will oppose any attempt by the state to commit genocide against older people. Age shouldn't be the criteria that determines treatment and care, it should be the *chances of continued human function*. If an operation for a 70-year-old or a 20-year-old has only a one out of 100 chance to enable them continued function in a human way— maybe it shouldn't be done. Our medical resources should not be wasted when there is no hope of real human life at either end of life.

Health Care Resources

The rationing of health care resources poses difficult ethical questions at either end of life. How will society put limits on care?

I was on the LORAN commission—(named after the submarine underwater guiding device of World War II) set up by the Harvard Community Health Plan to come up with a set of principles with which to decide whether or not HMOs [health maintenance organizations], a prototype for managed care, would cover new high-tech developments like artificial livers, and on what principles they would make these technologies available.

It clearly wasn't fair to endanger the limited resources of any "health maintenance organization" by spending millions or even hundreds of thousands of dollars on new, big ticket, high-technology procedures that might or might not give one or a few otherwise dead individuals a few more months or years of life, of what quality? But how, indeed, to make such life-and-death distinctions? These questions were particularly critical at the two ends of life, after birth and near death. Already, far too high a proportion of America's exploding health care bill is being spent on neonatal and terminal care, keeping alive premature babies and dying elders with no real hope of developing or sustaining full human capacity.

We clearly need to develop a new morality. To that end, we have made some progress in expanding the living will and the hospice. Today, far too many older people still become depersonalized, passive, objects of "care" with prolonged, medical intervention. At a certain point when a person's cancer is not curable and there is no hope that any kind of cure would enable that person to function in a good human way, they might refuse to endure more pain futilely. They may decide against more chemotherapy, intervention and the depletion of family resources and choose to approach death as a reality of life. A hospice would enable that person to die in as much comfort and in as little pain as possible with family and friends around.

The Boundaries of Life

In another time the Hippocratic tradition defined the doctor's realm as between the two edges of life—after quickening and before the agony of death. How will we determine these extreme ends of life today?

The LORAN commission drafted a consensus on "Limits of Health Care at the Extreme Ends of Life." We didn't get very far—but we could agree on the "brain death" criteria to determine death (not heartbeat or vegetative life). We could recommend as a current guideline that "no delivered conceptus shall be sustained if it weighs 600 grams or less *and* is 24 weeks or younger, since, at this time, even when extensive costly measures are taken, fewer than one percent of such deliveries survive" and only a fraction of them in anything like a whole state. But as to "issues surrounding the end of life," all we could agree on was an educational program around the concept of the living will to provide people with the means of defining the limits of their lives *as they wish them to be.*

We recommended that all hospitals and health plans have an ethics or review committee made up of people from medicine, law, and philosophy as a body to which patient's family members can turn as a last resort in making decisions about sustaining human existence when terminal or irreversible illness or injury makes recovery unlikely. We also thought such a committee should be guided by some version of calculus which seeks to take into account all the factors by which life can be measured and defined.

Beyond that, the Hippocratic tradition in a way lends a definition of the boundaries of human life—from quickening to the agony of death. Life ends with death and the human being is not human before the human being is born. And in all the intervening period, what defines our humanness is our ability to choose, to love and to work. The real goal of health care, then, is to maximize our human function at any period of life and at no period of human life should we treat human patients in a way that denies them their own personhood, dignity or autonomy of choice. This human life ends in death, death is a part of life and we should retain our maximum dignity and our choice in death.

Breaking the Mystique of Age

These are the principles that we must embrace personally and socially. If we begin to break through the dread mystique of age, we discover that the programmed deterioration turns out not to be true. For people aging in the community, decline doesn't happen now until well into their 80s or just before death, and for some there is no decline or even new growth and generativity. More than any other time of life, in age decline or generativity depends on what you do and don't do. When we break through the obsession with youth and the denial of age, then we can begin to deal with the reality of this new third of life and its termination in death, and we will deal with it simply as a part of our whole human existence.

"Employers continue to view age not in terms of experience or stability but as deterioration and staleness."

Companies Are Biased Against Older Workers

Esther B. Fein

Workers over age fifty-five have increasing difficulty gaining jobs and acceptance among America's employers, Esther B. Fein contends in the following viewpoint. According to experts and displaced workers interviewed by Fein, employers are disregarding the proven abilities of older workers and discriminating against them simply because of their age. Fein is a reporter for the *New York Times* daily newspaper.

As you read, consider the following questions:

1. According to Fein, how much did unemployment among older workers increase between 1987 and 1992?
2. Why do many workers accept early retirement, according to Fein?
3. What are some euphemisms for "you're too old," according to job seekers interviewed by the author?

Despite a decade-long push by private and government organizations to market older people as reliable and mature workers, advocates for people 55 and older say their efforts have largely failed. They say that employers continue to view age not in terms of experience or stability but as deterioration and staleness.

People who have worked to promote the older labor force say that in the mid-1980s they were confident that, through intensive public relations and educational efforts, American businesses would recognize and harness what they argued are the skills of older workers. Although it is impossible to tally how much money went toward that end, people who work in the field estimated that tens of millions of dollars were spent nationwide on studies, job fairs, seminars for executives and advertising.

Libby Mandel is 69 years old and has been looking for a job for two years. She has taken advantage of many of these programs, going to computer classes, résumé writing workshops and job fairs, and thrusting herself forward as an experienced secretary who had, for 25 years, skillfully handled the paper, telephone and student traffic at Seward Park High School in New York City.

"These senior programs were all supposed to show people that age doesn't matter," said Mrs. Mandel, in a voice more resigned than hopeful. "But it does. It still does. It's like a handicap. Really."

Anger and Frustration

Now people running these programs, as well as older workers themselves, say they are frustrated and angry at how little headway they have made in changing attitudes and hiring practices.

To be sure, all agree, the recession has not helped. But in many cases, they say, the burden of age in the job market is as profound as those of race and gender.

The Federal Age Discrimination in Employment Act, which was enacted in 1967 and amended several times since, prohibits any form of discrimination in the workplace due to a person's age. The law now eliminates mandatory retirement ages for all but very select positions, including top-level executives.

Employers may not ask a job applicant's age or consider it when making a hiring decision, except where it is a so-called "bona fide occupational qualification." An example of that would be a job like construction, where physical strength is an issue, but even then a fit and robust older worker would be protected. The fact that a job is entry level or that a company envisions training someone for a longterm career track would be irrelevant to the law.

But it is too often relevant to employers, complain advocates for older workers, although proving age discrimination in em-

189

ployment is very difficult.

People like Mrs. Mandel, who have journeyed futilely about the job market, say that they can actually feel themselves dissolve from vital individuals into antique stereotypes as they sit before interviewers who, careful not to run afoul of discrimination laws, try surreptitiously to find out applicants' ages and couch their biases in the most deferential terms.

"When I look at myself, I see a funny person basically, a helper; I'm enthusiastic," Mrs. Mandel said. "But when I talk to these recruiters or go on interviews, I know what they see is an old lady. They don't have to see my date of birth. They see the gray hair, they see the wrinkles, and they think, 'Old.'"

Dire Statistics

The job market, while showing some recent signs of recovery, is still a grim odyssey for most unemployed people, but it is particularly so for older people. Statistically, the situation for older workers in the New York region is significantly worse than the country as a whole. Nationwide in 1992, about 738,000 people age 55 and older were unemployed and actively looking for jobs, a rise of about 51 percent in five years, according to the Bureau of Labor Statistics. In the New York area, those ranks swelled nearly 2½ times in the same period—from 28,000 to 67,000—due, in large measure to the corporate reorganization that took place here in the 1980's and the subsequent recession.

Still, the jobless rate for older workers—4.8 percent in the United States and 6.8 percent in the New York region in 1992—is lower than that of the general work force. But experts say those figures reflect the stability of workers who have had steady jobs and have not been forced back into the marketplace. The numbers also don't reflect older workers who, put off by dismal prospects, have stopped looking for jobs.

Weeding Out Older Workers

There are, to be sure, some companies that have responded and have reached out to aging workers. But experts say that the "untapped resource," as one report referred to workers 55 years and older, remains largely that—untapped.

"I wish I could say that because of all these case studies companies are running out in droves to hire older workers," said Michael Barth, a labor economist and senior vice president for ICF, a Washington consulting firm that specializes in labor market studies. "But if anything, they are finding more ways to get rid of them and the reason is because there is a lot of pure bias, of behaving toward older workers totally in the context of their age, not their ability."

People 55 and older are increasingly looking for jobs for many reasons. People are living longer and healthier and have a desire and ability to keep active professionally for longer.

In addition, in a period of massive corporate layoffs and downsizing, older workers are frequently induced into taking early retirement, afraid that if they don't accept severance packages one year, they will be let go without any safety net the following year. But the money is usually not enough for them to live on, considering average life expectancy and a troubled economy.

Studies Offer Praise

A variety of studies—some of which surveyed human resources executives at hundreds of firms, others of which focused on particular companies—have found that workers age 55 and older are more reliable, have lower rates of absenteeism, higher productivity and were just as easy to retrain as their younger colleagues.

But the prejudices against older workers are so ingrained, people who have studied the issue say, they defy logic and hard data.

Encounter with Discrimination

I know that ageism in the form of job discrimination exists because I have encountered it. For many years, I worked in some phase of the publishing industry, as researcher, writer and copy editor. When I was younger, I received so many offers from publishing companies that I was forced to turn down assignments. But when I reached retirement age, the assignments began to fall off even though I indicated that I wanted to continue working and my work was generally commended. Simply put, when it came to a choice between me and a young person of equal qualifications, the younger person won out almost every time.

Bernice Balfour, *Los Angeles Times*, December 13, 1995.

"In the beginning, I was more optimistic that if we corrected the stereotype, if we could document productivity, that it would help change attitudes," said Karen Davis, the executive vice president of the Commonwealth Fund, a private foundation based in New York that completed a five-year, $4 million study of workers over 55. "I really thought the reports would have had more of a positive impact. But we are running against the economic trends and some deep-rooted bias. I still think it may turn around but it's clearly going to be an uphill struggle to make it happen."

At a job fair for older workers at the Roosevelt Hotel in Manhattan—promisingly named "Ability is Ageless"—participants walked from booth to booth, leaving their résumés with recruiters and commiserating with each other about the indignities of job-hunting at their age.

New Yorkers Handle the Age Question

"I'm ashamed to admit it, but I dye my hair, like a lady, to give myself a more youthful appearance," said one man, a 62-year-old former salesman from Flushing who declined to give his name. "And I wear bright ties. They should think I'm with it, and not stuffy." He fingered a yellow swath of silk with aqua crests and sighed, "So far, it hasn't helped."

Similar laments are repeated at job fairs in other cities and at workshops and training programs designed to make aging workers more competitive. At AgeWorks, a 16-week skills-improvement course run by the New York City Department for the Aging, several women compared euphemisms for "you're too old" that they had encountered in their job quests.

"They say that you're overqualified, even if you're willing to take a lower-level job," said Sara Lerner, a former bookkeeper from Riverdale, who, like many people interviewed, would give her name, but not her age.

"That's the main one they use," said Karen Halpern, who was given early retirement recently from her job at I.B.M.

"There's also, 'I'd love to hire you, but you just won't fit in,'" said Helen Miller, of Ridgewood, Queens, who was candid about her 66 years and is looking for clerical work. "They also get around asking you your age by asking what year you graduated, or asking to see your driver's license."

If they do get hired, many older workers find that it is for a job that is far lower in pay and stature than their previous position.

For 25 years Cecil Frazier was a chef at the Gloucester House, a pricey midtown restaurant where he was known for his lobster bisque. Now he grills burgers and fries chicken for a T.G.I. Friday's restaurant in Manhattan, and in spite of that drop in status, he is grateful.

Most of the people he worked with before the Gloucester House closed in 1992 are still looking for work, their years of experience proving no lure to potential employers. "They're working 20 years and more and can't get no jobs," said Mr. Frazier, who is 60 and searched nearly a year before finding work. "But the younger guys, now they got the jobs. They've got no experience, but they got the jobs."

Dr. Marjorie Honig, professor of the economics department at Hunter College, said the problems of prejudice encountered by older workers were similar to those faced by women and minority groups. "It's not reasonable, but it's there," she said.

"Businesses will be paying more attention to the problems and concerns of older consumers."

Businesses Value Older Consumers

Kenneth J. Doka

Businesses recognize the importance of older consumers as a growing and affluent market for their products and services, Kenneth J. Doka maintains in the following viewpoint. Doka contends that companies are seeking to meet the demands of older consumers and to overcome barriers to this market group. Doka is a professor of gerontology at the College of New Rochelle in New York.

As you read, consider the following questions:

1. According to Doka, why do older consumers tend to have less in common with each other compared to younger people?
2. In the author's opinion, why are older people unreceptive to terms that reflect aging?
3. What did an airline discover about catering to older consumers, according to Doka?

Kenneth J. Doka, "When Gray Is Golden," *The Futurist*, July/August 1992. Reproduced with permission from *The Futurist*, published by the World Future Society, 7910 Woodmont Ave., Suite 450, Bethesda, MD 20814.

In the late 1950s, an entrepreneur named Perry Mendel recognized that the baby boom was producing an abundance of preschool children. He also realized that many women, including the mothers of these children, were interested in returning to work. Seeing an unmet and growing need for quality child care, Mendel founded Kinder-Care Learning Centers. Three decades later, the company grossed over $1.25 billion during 1990 alone.

Kinder-Care's success in capitalizing on a major demographic shift is a valuable lesson, and many businesses today are beginning to view the next major shift—the aging of America—with great interest. Older Americans will want and need different services and products than younger people. The businesses that can effectively meet those needs may realize profits that will make Kinder-Care's success seem like child's play.

A simple analogy illustrates the changing business climate. Imagine a community where most of the residents comprise young parents and their children. The stores and services that this community might offer include toy stores, recreational activities, day care, and day camps. Now imagine that this community has suddenly aged: A high proportion of its residents are over 65, but the mix of stores and services remains pretty much the same. The first stores that catered to the town's new older adults might gain a substantial number of loyal customers.

A Powerful Market

Almost 12% of the U.S. population is now 65 or older. By 2025, when most baby boomers will have reached retirement age, older Americans will outnumber teenagers by a 2-to-1 ratio.

If one adds to this population those "near old"—that is, 50-to 64-year-olds—the size of the mature market becomes truly astounding. Americans over 50 have combined incomes of more than $800 billion. They hold 51% of all discretionary income in the United States, accounting for 40% of consumer demand. They own almost half of the luxury cars in the country, over a third of the spa and health-club memberships, and over three-quarters of the dollars in savings. Mark Zitter of Age Wave, Inc., a firm that advises business and government on the implications of an aging society, has called this new awareness of the spending power of mature Americans "the demographic discovery of the decade."

Yet, this vast market cannot be taken for granted; older people will not purchase goods or services that they don't want. Businesses are beginning to recognize the complex nature of this market, the barriers they will face, and ways they can be more sensitive to the needs of older consumers.

Businesses are learning that there is no one great gray marketplace, but rather a number of different markets. Mature consumers are highly heterogeneous, differing by family and marital status, ethnicity, geography, education, and social class. In fact, older Americans probably have less in common with each other than do younger people, since a higher proportion of seniors where born abroad. They also lack the unifying culture that television provided for later generations.

Another variable is age itself. For example, the "young-old" are far more likely to be interested in travel and leisure services than are the "old-old."

George Mochis, director of Georgia State University's Center for Mature Consumer Studies, believes that two criteria are essential for understanding older consumers: health, and what he describes as extroversion-introversion, meaning that some seniors are private and home centered while others are more interested in socializing and and traveling. From these two variables, Mochis divides older Americans into four categories.

Types of Older Consumers

	Extroverted	Introverted
In good health	Healthy Indulgers (healthy, active): 13% Interested in financial services, clothes, entertainment, leisure services, high-technology items	Healthy Hermits (healthy but home centered): 38% Interested in home entertainment, domestic services, home conveniences, do-it-yourself items
In poor health	Ailing Outgoers (active but ailing, health conscious): 34% Interested in retirement housing and health services	Frail Recluses (failing health, home centered): 15% Interested in domestic assistance, home and health services, home-based entertainment

Source: George Mochis, Center for Mature Consumer Studies, Georgia State University.

A range of businesses can expect to gain from an aging population, says Jeff Ostroff, a vice president of Data Group, Inc. These businesses include:

1. Home products. Since many older consumers' lives are centered in their homes, products that offer luxury, convenience, or security may find a ready market. These include security systems, home entertainment systems, comfort items such as air conditioning, and housekeeping, repair, and maintenance services.

2. Health care. Most older consumers will face minor or major health problems. They will need prescription and over-the-counter drugs, corrective devices such as hearing aids, and a variety of health-related services such as home health care, adult day care, respite care, and nursing home care.

3. *Wellness and youth-enhancing products.* America may be aging, but many older consumers want to look and feel as young as possible. Products and services that will be in demand include exercise equipment, health-club memberships, and weight-control products; foods low in cholesterol or salt; vitamins; and products that mask or retard aging such as cosmetics (Porcelana), hair coloring, and skin moisturizers (Oil of Olay).

4. *Recreational and leisure services.* While some mature consumers are home centered, many enjoy travel and entertainment away from home. There will be great opportunities for hotels, travel services, restaurants, and entertainment and hospitality services in general. Twenty-three hotel chains offer discounts to members of the American Association of Retired Persons.

5. *Financial services and products.* Many mature consumers have considerable funds to invest. Financial advisement, investment seminars, and financial products can tap that demand.

6. *Educational services.* The need to learn and grow never stops, and older consumers have the time to indulge intellectual interests. A range of educational services will prove appealing, from educational travel such as Elderhostel (an international organization that provides low-cost housing and "mini courses" at college campuses) to community education to credit-bearing programs aimed at preparing older people for second careers.

7. *Business consulting.* Many older consumers, though retired, wish to continue putting their skills to use or to develop new skills. This will create opportunities for business and employment services for second or third careers.

These businesses can expect to benefit the most from the aging of America, but other businesses will also find opportunities. Toy manufacturers, for example, may consider advertising aimed at grandparents. The television and movie industries will be more aware of these changing demographics and the potential for some films to bring a new viewing audience. Appealing "new" mature heroes and heroines have already emerged in films like *Cocoon* and *Driving Miss Daisy* and TV shows like *The Golden Girls*, *Matlock*, and *Murder, She Wrote*. Supermarkets may revise their inventory and adjust the portions and even the ways they package meats in order to gain a better slice of the great gray marketplace.

Barriers to the Mature Market

Though opportunities for all types of businesses abound, formidable barriers exist as well. The biggest barrier is psychological. One of the most effective ways to alienate older consumers is to aim explicitly for them.

A number of years ago, a company wanted to start a book club for older adults. Research indicated that older Americans had both the time and interest to read. The company would offer editions in large print or on cassette tape, and it had a good grasp of the types of literature adults desired. Yet, the club had a short life: Few people would identify with a book club for older readers.

Despite an aging population, American society remains obsessed with youth. Terms that reflect aging still have negative connotations, even to the elderly. Few want to identify with a product that is for "old people." An organization once asked me what would be the most acceptable term to older consumers. Would they prefer to be called "golden agers," "mature," "elderly," or some other term? The truth is that *no* term reflecting age will be appreciated by the elderly.

A Significant Margin of the Consumer Base

While a lot of research is done on the 55-plus group, relatively little information is available on the packaging requirements of the mature consumer. Seventy percent of those surveyed buy books frequently; 62% buy cosmetics and fragrances and over-the-counter pharmaceuticals and vitamins. So we know they are well-read, well-off, they like to look good, and they enjoy "treats" and luxuries. By designing largely to the youth market or the 18–35 age group, we may be losing a significant margin of the overall consumer base.

Charles Biondo, quoted in *USA Today*, April 1995.

Part of the reason is that most older people feel younger than they actually are. Most 65-year-olds, for example, say they feel more like 55-year-olds. "Older," then, is always a label applied to someone else.

Businesses are adopting a number of strategies to avoid this barrier. One approach is to be age irrelevant. In this way, a company can identify with the concerns and needs of older Americans without identifying these concerns as old. For example, a frozen-food company may emphasize that its products are low in sodium—often a concern of seniors worried about high blood pressure—without specifically identifying them as products for old people.

Another approach is to establish affinity with older consumers by using older spokespersons. In a series of Coca Cola commercials, for example, Art Carney portrayed a grandfather of a clearly adoring young grandson. Carney was clever and sprightly as he and his grandson shared a Coke. The message was unstated, yet clear: Coke is a drink for all generations.

There is another barrier to the great gray marketplace. Older consumers are both cautious and careful. They have been consumers for a long time and at times when companies were less scrupulous in their advertising than they are now. They have the time to gather and evaluate information, and so are less likely to buy on impulse. In short, older consumers are smart shoppers.

And they are loyal. Over time, they have learned to trust certain brands, stores, and sales and service persons. They are not likely to change without good reason. In return, they demand a certain loyalty and consistency. A study by Mochis found that older consumers were less likely than younger consumers to complain to manufacturers or regulators. They were, however, more likely to simply switch products, services, or stores.

Businesses will attempt to overcome these barriers by combining needed products and services with effective marketing strategies, such as providing easy-to-read print or toll-free telephone numbers for more information. But there is often a cost to success. It is possible that a product or service identified with older consumers may find itself less desirable to other consumers. In addition, older consumers may have distinct needs that require different models of service.

One major airline serves as a good illustration of both points. Several years ago, the airline began targeting older travelers, even creating a special travel "club." These efforts have been successful, but now the airline is concerned that the number of older consumers in the business-class section may change the "feel" of that section and make it less attractive to regular business customers.

In addition, when older consumers call the reservation lines, they tend to want to compare times, discuss trip plans, and evaluate options. But this slows down the ticketing process for reservation clerks, who are evaluated on their speed. The airline thus had to create an additional phone line with specially trained clerks for the travel club.

Seeing Through Seniors' Eyes

Businesses that hope to gain the favor of older consumers must learn to take their perspective, suggests Ken Dychtwald, author of *Age Wave*. They must see the world as the older consumer does.

Thus, businesses will be paying more attention to the problems and concerns of older consumers. One of the standard sensitivity exercises in gerontology classes is to simulate the disabilities that sometimes plague the elderly: Reducing mobility, dexterity, or sense abilities often helps potential caregivers empathize with older clients. Businesses may increasingly use similar techniques to aid in product design.

Cars designed for older people, says Dychtwald, might feature swivel chairs, brightly illuminated dashboards with larger print, and easy-to-manipulate levers. Clothes may use Velcro instead of small, hard-to-handle buttons. Houses for seniors could allow easier access and provide safety and security features.

Businesses will also be taking note of older consumers' interests, such as what sorts of music, movies, and travel experiences they enjoy. Many older travelers have already toured all the common sites. Travel companies might entice these worldly tourists by providing easy and convenient access: The trip would begin with a limousine ride to the airport, and all baggage, transfers, and check-ins would be conveniently handled. Or the trip could provide ongoing stimulation, such as a tour of the wine country of France led by a wine expert. Unusual experiences, such as a trip on the *Concorde* [airliner], might also attract the older traveler.

Technology

Older consumers' attitudes toward technology will be taken into greater consideration. Although older people have the reputation of being "technology averse," Mochis has found that they are no less likely than younger consumers to adapt to new technologies if they understand a given innovation and can see the benefit of owning it. Thus, a store that sells VCRs might offer installation and instruction to older buyers. Providing a VCR or a computer to a senior center may be as good an investment as providing computers to schools proved to be.

And businesses will be paying heed to the needs of their own aging employees. New laws that have ended mandatory retirement have created a demand for comprehensive pre-retirement counseling programs. In addition, adult employees with older parents will need such services as elder care, information and referral, and case management.

In retrospect, the concept of Kinder-Care seems so obvious. But Mendel was the first to see in the demographics of the baby boom a great opportunity and to seize it. The new demographic reality, the aging of America, will provide similar opportunities for businesses sensitive to the needs of older people.

Periodical Bibliography

The following articles have been selected to supplement the diverse views presented in this chapter. Addresses are provided for periodicals not indexed in the *Readers' Guide to Periodical Literature*, the *Alternative Press Index*, or the *Social Sciences Index*.

Bernice Balfour	"The Indignity of Being Old," *Los Angeles Times*, December 13, 1995. Available from Reprints, Times Mirror Square, Los Angeles, CA 90012-3816.
Mark Clements	"What We Say About Aging," *Parade*, December 12, 1993. Available from 711 Third Ave., New York, NY 10017.
Katherine Dowling	"Seniors Should Still Do Their Fair Share," *U.S. Catholic*, August 1993.
Linda Ellerbee	"Should We—Must We—Lie About Our Age?" *New Choices for Retirement Living*, September 1995.
Suzanne Fields	"Twilight Years in the Twilight Zone," *Conservative Chronicle*, April 22, 1992. Available from PO Box 29, Hampton, IA 50441.
Constance L. Hays	"If the Hair Is Gray, Con Artists See Green," *New York Times*, May 21, 1995.
Susan E. Kuhn	"Retire Today—Find a New Job Tomorrow," *Fortune*, July 24, 1995.
Mark S. Lachs and Karl Pillemer	"Abuse and Neglect of Elderly Persons," *New England Journal of Medicine*, February 16, 1995. Available from 10 Shattuck St., Boston, MA 02115-6094.
Doron P. Levin	"The Graying Factory," *New York Times*, February 20, 1994.
Abigail McCarthy	"Keep on Truckin'," *Commonweal*, July 14, 1995.
Jon Nordheimer	"A New Abuse of Elderly: Theft by Kin and Friends," *New York Times*, December 16, 1991.
Cynthia M. Taeuber	"Women in Our Aging Society: Golden Years or Increased Dependency?" *USA Today*, September 1993.

For Further Discussion

Chapter 1

1. Charles F. Longino Jr. contends that factors such as improved health, new ways of providing health care, and improved technology will reduce disability among the elderly and lengthen the average person's life. Michael D'Antonio argues that while more elderly Americans will live longer, they will face the financial burden of supporting themselves for additional years of life. As an elderly person, would you choose to live longer knowing that you faced financial hardship? Why or why not?

2. Laurence J. Kotlikoff and Jagadeesh Gokhale argue that future generations of Americans will pay a higher percentage of taxes than past or present elderly citizens. What does Robert Eisner write about the benefits that will be gained by future Americans? Whose argument is more convincing, and why?

Chapter 2

1. Alan Simpson, who is old enough to qualify for Social Security benefits, is a member of the U.S. Senate's Special Committee on Aging. Richard Thau, in his thirties, is the executive director of Third Millennium, an advocacy organization concerned with issues that affect younger Americans. How might their ages and professions influence their opinions about Social Security? How does knowing their backgrounds affect your assessment of their viewpoints, if at all?

2. William G. Shipman advocates allowing workers to invest part of their earnings in stocks and bonds rather than deducting taxes for Social Security from their pay. Horace Deets warns that by doing so, workers would bear the risk of their investments. Based on your reading of these viewpoints, do you believe that workers would benefit more from such private investment? Why or why not?

Chapter 3

1. In their viewpoint, Florence Tauber and Al Tauber advocate working past the retirement age of sixty-five. By doing so, they argue, older workers will benefit from continued earnings and avoid suffering from a loss of self-esteem. In what other ways can such workers benefit, in your opinion? Can you think of any disadvantages? Explain your answers.

2. Leslie Eaton cites a variety of studies and surveys to support her argument that many future retirees will face financial hardship. Identify these sources of information and rank them according to how effectively each supports Eaton's argument.

Chapter 4

1. Lou L. Hartney defends her decision to place her aged mother in a nursing home by describing her mother's activities and friendship with a roommate. Betty Friedan criticizes nursing homes for neglecting patients and having filthy living conditions. Which author's argument is more persuasive? Why?

2. Daniel Callahan writes that attempts to conquer aging-related diseases are likely to be very expensive. As America's elderly population increases, do you believe that billions of dollars should be spent in this endeavor? Why or why not? Are there other needs that you think society should address instead? Explain.

Chapter 5

1. Jere Daniel contends that the media reinforce a negative view of aging. Do you believe that the media tend to portray old age negatively or positively? Use examples to support your answer.

2. What words does Nancy J. Osgood use to compare the differences between youth and old age? Make a list of similar words that could be used to describe youth and old age.

3. Esther B. Fein cites the strength required of construction workers as a characteristic that could preclude older workers. Can you think of other jobs in which older workers might not be suited? What would make it difficult for older workers to perform these jobs? What jobs would be appropriate for elderly workers?

Organizations to Contact

The editors have compiled the following list of organizations concerned with the issues debated in this book. The descriptions are derived from materials provided by the organizations. All have publications or information available for interested readers. The list was compiled on the date of publication of the present volume; names, addresses, and phone numbers, fax numbers, and e-mail addresses may change. Be aware that many organizations take several weeks or longer to respond to inquiries, so allow as much time as possible.

Alzheimer's Association
919 N. Michigan Ave., Suite 1000
Chicago, IL 60611-1676
(800) 272-3900

The association is a national nonprofit organization dedicated to education, care, and research concerning Alzheimer's disease. Services include health counseling, a speakers bureau, and self-help and support groups led by trained facilitators. It publishes the quarterly *National Newsletter* and an information packet.

American Association of Retired Persons (AARP)
601 E St. NW
Washington, DC 20049
(202) 434-2277
fax: (202) 434-2320

AARP, with more than thirty million members, is the largest advocacy group of Americans over the age of fifty. It seeks to improve every aspect of living for older people and focuses on concerns such as health care and pensions. AARP is committed to preserving the federal Social Security and Medicare programs. The association publishes the monthly newsletter *AARP News Bulletin*, the bimonthly newsletter *Working Age*, and the bimonthly magazine *Modern Maturity*.

American Geriatrics Society (AGS)
770 Lexington Ave., Suite 300
New York, NY 10021
(212) 308-1414
fax: (212) 832-8646

AGS is a for-profit professional society of physicians and other health care professionals interested in the aged. It encourages and promotes the study of geriatrics and stresses the importance of medical research in the field of aging. Publications include the bimonthly *AGS Newsletter* and the monthly *Journal of the American Geriatrics Society*.

American Health Care Association (AHCA)
1201 L St. NW
Washington, DC 20005
(202) 842-4444
fax: (202) 842-3860

AHCA is a federation of state associations of long-term health care facilities. It promotes standards for professionals in long-term health care delivery and quality care for patients and residents in a safe environment. AHCA publishes the monthly newsletter *AHCA Notes*.

American Society on Aging (ASA)
833 Market St., Suite 511
San Francisco, CA 94103-1824
(415) 974-9600
fax: (415) 882-4280

ASA is an organization of health care and social service professionals, educators, researchers, administrators, businesspersons, students, and senior citizens working to enhance the well-being of older individuals. Its publications include the bimonthly newspaper *Aging Today* and the quarterly journal *Generations*.

Coalition of Advocates for the Rights of the Infirm Elderly (CARIE)
1315 Walnut St., Suite 1000
Philadelphia, PA 19107
(215) 545-5728
fax: (215) 545-5372

CARIE is a nonprofit organization dedicated to improving the quality of life for older adults, protecting their rights, promoting an awareness of their needs, and ensuring that necessary services are made available. Its Home Care Advocacy Project works on behalf of vulnerable older adults who receive long-term care services in their homes or communities and promotes their maximum independence. CARIE publishes the quarterly *CARIE Newsletter* and the pamphlets *Do You Need Help at Home?* and *Who Can Stop Elder Abuse?*

Foundation Aiding the Elderly (FATE)
PO Box 254849
Sacramento, CA 95865-4849
(916) 481-8558

The foundation assists individuals with relatives and friends in long-term-care nursing homes. It provides awareness of the existence of, and potential for, abuse, neglect, and loss of dignity of the elderly in nursing homes. FATE advocates and raises funds for legislation to bring about nursing home reform. Its publications include an information sheet and a newsletter.

Gray Panthers
2025 Pennsylvania Ave. NW, Suite 821
Washington, DC 20006
(202) 466-3132
fax: (202) 466-3133

Gray Panthers is a consciousness-raising activist group of older adults and young people that aims to combat ageism—the discrimination against persons on the basis of chronological age. It believes that both the old and the young have much to contribute to make our society more just and humane. The organization publishes the monthly *Network Newsletter* and the semiannual *Gray Panther Network* newsletter.

International Federation on Ageing (IFA)
380 St. Antoine St. W, Suite 3200
Montreal, PQ H2Y 3X7
CANADA
(514) 287-9679
fax: (514) 987-1567

IFA is a federation of voluntary organizations from many countries that acts as an advocate for the elderly. It exchanges information on aging on an international level and assists in the creation of associations of the aging. IFA publishes the quarterly journal *Ageing International*, the monthly *IFA Newsletter*, handbooks, monographs, and reports.

International Society for Retirement Planning (ISRP)
833 Market St., Suite 511
San Francisco, CA 94103-1824
(415) 974-9631
fax: (415) 974-0300

ISRP is an organization of personnel directors, financial planners, and consultants that acts as a clearinghouse for preretirement counseling and planning programs. It publishes the quarterly newsletter *Perspectives on Retirement* and the quarterly journal *Retirement Planning*.

National Association for Home Care (NAHC)
519 C St. NE
Washington, DC 20002-5809
(202) 547-7424
fax: (202) 547-3540

NAHC is an association of providers of home health care and hospice services. It develops and promotes high standards of patient care in home care services. NAHC publications include the monthly magazine *Caring*, the monthly tabloid *Homecare News*, and the weekly newsletter *NAHC Report*.

National Council of Senior Citizens (NCSC)
1331 F St. NW
Washington, DC 20004-1171
(202) 347-8800
fax: (202) 624-9595

NCSC is an organization of autonomous senior citizen associations, clubs, councils, and other groups. The council is an educational and action group that supports the preservation of Medicare and Social Security, the enactment of a national health plan that includes long-term care, reduced costs on drugs, better housing, and other programs to aid senior citizens. NCSC publishes the *Senior Citizens News* and *Retirement Newsletter* monthly.

National Council on the Aging (NCOA)
409 Third St. SW, 2nd Fl.
Washington, DC 20024
(202) 479-1200
fax: (202) 479-0735

The council consists of individuals and organizations working on behalf of older Americans and promotes concern for them. It conducts research and programs on issues important to older people, such as training and placement of older workers, economic security, home services for the frail elderly, and access to health and social services. NCOA publishes the bimonthly newspaper *NCOA Networks* and the quarterly magazine *Perspective on Aging*.

National Institute on Age, Work, and Retirement (NIAWR)
c/o National Council on the Aging
409 Third St. SW, Suite 200
Washington, DC 20024
(202) 479-1200
fax: (202) 479-0735

NIAWR promotes opportunities for middle-aged and older workers and conducts research on work/retirement behavior and attitudes. The institute provides information on organizations serving older workers, offers technical assistance to older-worker program directors, and advises corporations on employment practices and retirement planning programs. Its publications include the quarterly newsletter *Business Newsline* and the book *Aging and Competition: Rebuilding the U.S. Workforce*.

National Institute on Aging Information Center (NIA)
PO Box 8057
Gaithersburg, MD 20898-8057
(301) 496-1752
fax: (301) 589-3014

NIA is part of the National Institutes of Health. The institute conducts and supports biomedical, social, and behavioral research to increase the knowledge of the aging process and associated physical, psychological, and social factors resulting from advanced age. Its special areas of study include Alzheimer's disease, memory loss, menopause, and susceptibility to diseases. NIA publishes the fact sheets *Health Resources for Older Women*, *Answers About Aging*, and *When You Need a Nursing Home*.

Seniors Coalition
11166 Main St., Suite 302
Fairfax, VA 22030
(703) 591-0663
fax: (703) 591-0679

The coalition opposes Social Security reforms that would penalize seniors. It asserts that the problem lies not in Social Security benefits or payroll taxes but in out-of-control federal spending. Seniors Coalition supports Republican measures for Medicare reform that emphasize consumer choice of competing private health plans. The organization publishes the bimonthly newspaper *Senior Class*.

Third Millennium
817 Broadway, 6th Fl.
New York, NY 10003
212-979-2001
e-mail: thirdmil@reach.com

Third Millennium is an organization of young adults concerned about America's future. The group argues that while most Americans of retirement age are satisfied with Social Security, many young adults have little confidence in the system's viability. Third Millennium contends that this difference could be the basis for increased intergenerational conflict. Its publications include the quarterly newsletter *Future Focus*.

Bibliography of Books

Jessie Allen and Alan Pifer	*Women on the Front Lines: Meeting the Challenge of an Aging America*. Washington, DC: Urban Institute Press, 1994.
Merna J. Alpert	*The Chronically Disabled Elderly in Society*. Westport, CT: Greenwood, 1994.
American Association of Retired Persons, Research Division	*Aging Baby Boomers: How Secure Is Their Economic Future?* Washington, DC: AARP, 1994.
Robert L. Barry and Gerard V. Bradley	*Set No Limits: A Rebuttal to Daniel Callahan's Proposal to Limit Health Care for the Elderly*. Champaign: University of Illinois Press, 1991.
Phillip L. Berman and Connie Goldman, eds.	*The Ageless Spirit*. New York: Ballantine Books, 1992.
Thomas R. Cole	*The Journey of Life: A Cultural History of Aging in America*. Cambridge: Cambridge University Press, 1992.
Congressional Budget Office	*Baby Boomers in Retirement: An Early Perspective*. Washington, DC: Government Printing Office, September 1993.
Karen Ann Conner	*Aging America: Issues Facing an Aging Society*. Englewood Cliffs, NJ: Prentice-Hall, 1992.
Donna M. Corr and Charles A. Corr, eds.	*Nursing Care in an Aging Society*. New York: Springer, 1990.
Carole B. Cox	*The Frail Elderly: Problems, Needs, and Community Responses*. Westport, CT: Auburn House, 1993.
Peter Decalmer and Frank Glendenning	*The Mistreatment of Elderly People*. Newbury Park, CA: Sage, 1993.
Paula B. Doress-Worters and Diana Laskin Siegal	*The New Ourselves, Growing Older: Women Aging with Knowledge and Power*. New York: Touchstone, 1994.
Jeffrey A. Fisher	*Our Medical Future: Breakthroughs in Health, Medicine, and Longevity by the Year 2000 and Beyond*. New York: Pocket Books, 1992.
Irene A. Gutheil, ed.	*Work with Older People: Challenges and Opportunities*. New York: Fordham University Press, 1994.
Leonard Hayflick	*How and Why We Age*. New York: Ballantine Books, 1994.

Billie Jackson   *The Caregivers' Roller Coaster: A Practical Guide to Caregiving for the Frail Elderly*. Chicago: Loyola University Press, 1993.

Tom Koch   *A Place in Time: Care Givers for Their Elderly*. Westport, CT: Praeger, 1993.

Laurence J. Kotlikoff   *Generational Accounting: Knowing Who Pays, and When, for What We Spend*. New York: Free Press, 1992.

Walter N. Leutz et al.   *Care for Frail Elders: Developing Community Solutions*. Westport, CT: Auburn House, 1992.

Michael T. Levy   *Parenting Mom and Dad: A Guide for the Grown-up Children of Aging Parents*. New York: Prentice-Hall, 1991.

Barbara Logue   *Last Rights: Death Control and the Elderly in America*. New York: Lexington Books, 1993.

Abraham Monk   *Columbia Retirement Handbook*. New York: Columbia University Press, 1995.

Louis Mucciolo   *EightySomething: Interviews with Octogenarians Who Stay Involved*. New York: Carol Publishing Group, 1992.

Sherwin Nuland   *How We Die: Reflections on Life's Final Chapter*. New York: Knopf, 1994.

Ellen Olson,   *Controversies in Ethics in Long-Term Care*. New
Eileen R. Chichin,   York: Springer, 1995.
and Leslie S. Libow

Laura Katz Olson, ed.   *The Graying of the World: Who Will Care for the Frail Elderly?* New York: Haworth Press, 1994.

Richard A. Posner   *Aging and Old Age*. Chicago: University of Chicago Press, 1995.

Richard S. Prentis   *Passages of Retirement: Personal Histories of Struggle and Success*. Westport, CT: Greenwood, 1992.

Dallas L. Salisbury   *Retirement in the Twenty-first Century: Ready or
and Nora Super Jones   Not?* Washington, DC: Employee Benefit Research Institute, 1994.

Zalman Schachter-   *From Age-ing to Sage-ing: A Profound New Vision
Shalomi and   of Growing Older*. New York: Warner Books,
Ronald S. Miller   1995.

Kasturi Sen   *Ageing: Debates on Demographic Transition and Social Policy*. London: Zed Books, 1994.

Gail Sheehy   *New Passages: Mapping Your Life Across Time*. New York: Random House, 1995.

Jacob S. Siegel

A Generation of Change: A Profile of America's Older Population. New York: Russell Sage, 1993.

Page Smith

Old Age Is Another Country: A Traveler's Guide. Freedom, CA: Crossing Press, 1995.

C. Eugene Steuerle and Jon M. Bakija

Retooling Social Security for the Twenty-first Century: Right and Wrong Approaches to Reform. Washington, DC: Urban Institute Press, 1994.

Cynthia Taeuber and U.S. Bureau of the Census

Sixty-five Plus in America. Washington, DC: Government Printing Office, May 1993.

David Tilson, ed.

Aging in Place: Supporting the Frail Elderly in Residential Environments. Glenview, IL: Scott, Foresman, 1990.

Mark R. Wicclair

Ethics and the Elderly. New York: Oxford University Press, 1993.

Gerald R. Winslow and James W. Walters

Facing Limits: Ethics and Health Care for the Elderly. Boulder, CO: Westview, 1993.

John R. Wolfe

The Coming Health Crisis: How to Finance Care for the Aged in the Twenty-first Century. Chicago: University of Chicago Press, 1993.

Index

214